Kavanagh M.P.

an inspirational story

Kavanagh M.P.
an inspirational story

David Cohen

Psychology News Press

Published in 2005 by Psychology News Press

The publishers can be contacted at psychologynews@hotmail.com

Distribution and sales enquiries to melia@melia.org

Set in 11/14pt Garamond by Originator, Gt Yarmouth

ISBN 0907633048

Printed in Great Britain by Biddles Ltd, King's Lynn

Contents

Acknowledgements

The research into Kavanagh was supported by the Leverhulme Trust, which the author thanks.

This book would not exist but for the fact that Jane Eames, then my girlfriend, alerted me to his extraordinary history. We have lost touch but I wish to record my heart-felt thanks to her.

Reuben Cohen read the MS with great care and I wish to thank him for his acute critical comments as ever.

Andrew and Tina Kavanagh welcomed me to Borris and let me see many private papers. I thank them for their help.

Introduction:
How many limbs do you need to turn off the light?

When I started to learn about Arthur Kavanagh, I racked my brain for ways to imagine how one would cope with being as disabled as he was. I hope that what follows does not offend anyone who is disabled, but Arthur's disabilities were so extreme, an able-bodied author must try to understand as much as possible what it might have been like to live in his body.

One day I cut my fingers badly when I was shredding cabbage. It was an accident but I realised I had been handed a way of testing what it might be like to have no arms and no hands. I had a meeting to go to and I didn't want to leave the lights on in my house. How could I manage to turn off the lights without using my hands? Simple, I thought. I have a nose. I'll use it to press the light switches off. In practice, it wasn't quite so simple. Fingers are designed to grasp and manipulate objects. They're strong but the nose doesn't have a bone in it. A good hooter may be able to tell the difference between Chanel No 5 and Odour of Yves St Laurent but as an organ for switching domestic appliances off and on, the nose leaves a lot to be desired. As I was about to find out.

I stand in front of the light switch. I touch it with my nose. Too little pressure, the first time; so, the second time, I butt the bloody switch. Lights off, hooray. I will not rely on my nose to work the dishwasher.

I was feeling pleased with myself, when I realised I'd cheated. I'm 5′9″ tall, standing on my legs. But Arthur also had no legs.

Arthur Kavanagh was no more than 24 inches tall from head to toe – except that he had no feet and no toes. I couldn't imitate that, of course. The closest would be to get down on my knees.

If you kneel in front of a wall, you are nowhere near the height of normal light switches. If you have arms you can reach up for the switch but Arthur could not.

I wasn't going to give up. I was now running late. I got a chair and clambered up on it on my knees. I was a little too tall. I bent my head down very awkwardly and, at that angle, I couldn't get enough nose power to switch off the light.

I then found a box that wasn't so high. Now, finally, I was at a good working height. Balancing carefully on my knees on the box, I focussed. I rammed my nose against the switch.

It worked. Lights off. It had taken me 5 minutes to do something I usually do in a fraction of a second, without a moment's thought. As I've written this book, I've tried to remember my small experiment because I did not want to forget the obstacles Arthur faced from the moment he was born.

Chapter 1

The road to Borris

Borris House

Arthur's father, Thomas Kavanagh, had two children by his first marriage. His second wife, Harriett gave him two boys and a girl who were perfectly well. The baby she was carrying in 1830 would be her fourth child – and her last. The local doctor, Francis Boxwell spent a lot of time making sure Lady Harriett was comfortable. The Kavanaghs were not just local grandees, but one of the great families of Ireland. If they started to recommend Boxwell to their friends, his career would be made. He was 28 years old and had done nothing yet to distinguish himself. As Lady Harriett's pregnancy advanced, he was a little uneasy because he felt that the foetus was a little "displaced". But he could not give any more precise reason for his anxiety.

Giving birth was hazardous in the decade when Queen Victoria came to the throne. The poor were, of course, most at risk but hundreds of well-off young women also died in childbirth, or soon after. One of the most ironic deaths was that of Isabella Beeton, author of the great cookbook. She lost two sons when they were infants and, then, she died herself after giving birth to her fourth child. In *The Book of Household Management*, Isabella Beeton preached the necessity of hygiene but she got a fatal infection when she gave birth. The midwife had not obeyed the basic principles of hygiene.

If babies did come into the world safely, they were often lucky to survive much longer – sometimes because their own mothers murdered them. Thirty years after Arthur Kavanagh was born, this simmering concern about infant deaths peaked. In 1865, Esther

Lack murdered her three children by slitting their throats. Lack claimed she feared they would die of starvation. Doctors and lawyers excused her; her crime was attributed to "debility of constitution, caused by the delivery of three infants at a birth some seven or eight years ago." This provoked a "cynical response" from many papers. Every day, in every town, newborn children were found dead. The *Journal of Social Science* reported in 1866 that the police thought "no more of finding the dead body of a child in the street than picking up a dead dog or cat." Illegitimate babies were particularly at risk.

Dr Hilary Marland (2003) in her *Dangerous Motherhood* argues that severe post-natal depression afflicted record numbers of women in the 19th century. It accounted for up to 15 per cent of female asylum admissions. And these depressed mothers often disposed of their children. If they were brought to trial, they pleaded insanity. That was true both of unmarried girls, often in domestic service, and of married women who were said to have broken down under the strain of mothering.

Some babies were even flushed down the recently developed "crappers". Others were dumped in canals or left to die in the open. Babies who were born deformed were especially likely to be killed because they would be a financial burden.

The history of Arthur Kavanagh has to be seen against this macabre background.

The journey to Borris

In November 2000, I landed at Dublin airport and I had an hour to make the train to Bagnalstown, the nearest station to what still is the Kavanagh estate. It was raining heavily and three hundred people were queuing for taxis. There was no sign of the bus for Houston Street station. The only bus was the 377. I asked if it went anywhere near the station.

"I'll tell you where to get off," the driver said. "You can get a cab from there. I wouldn't panic. None of the trains are running," said the driver. "Floods. It's the worst weather we've had for years."

I had had to cancel one trip to Borris House because a close relative had died suddenly. On the phone the Irish Kavanaghs sounded pukka English. I imagined they would not be very pleased if I had to change the arrangements again.

"Do you mind taking me to Houston Street so I can check?" I said.

The railway station was deserted, the Irish railway system kaput. I went up to the ticket desk.

"Do you want a refund," said the clerk.

"I need to get to Bagnalstown."

"There are no trains today and probably no trains tomorrow." She seemed quite pleased; maybe there would never be trains again because, as well as the floods, the drivers were going on strike.

I walked back to the taxi. I had asked him to wait. "Would you take me to Bagnalstown?"

"It's two hours and you can see the floods."

I had expected to have to bargain.

"I couldn't do it for less than £100," the driver, Harry said.

"I've got £90 in my pocket," I said.

"I must be mad," Harry, the driver, said. "Why do you need to get there so badly?"

"Have you ever heard of Arthur MacMurrough Kavanagh?"

"Is he a jockey?"

I nearly said, "Well, he could ride and that was amazing enough."

"No, he wasn't a jockey," I replied.

I started to tell Harry something of Arthur's story. Harry was a good audience; he was duly amazed, and amazed he hadn't heard of Arthur. Arthur really does deserve more recognition than he's had.

We hit a total traffic jam ten miles out of Dublin. Harry turned off at the last moment to get on a small road. After that, the side roads threw up a few large puddles but nothing worse. It was a doddle compared to Arthur's travels. Two hours later, I handed over £90 in the small market town of Bagnalstown and rang Borris House.

Andrew Kavanagh had said he would come to pick me up. He was very friendly and astonished I'd arrived given the train strike. When he drove up to meet me, he was carrying a concrete mixer in

Borris House.

the back of his van. Before going to look at the archives, we had to get the mixer back to the shop he had rented it from.

From a distance, with its turrets, Borris House still looks impressive. The closer you get, the more you see its splendours are a bit ramshackle now. The yard is littered with ploughs, tractors, and other implements. As we parked at the back door, six or seven dogs barked wildly. I'm nervous of dogs but I did not want to make a bad impression so I put on my best "good dog, nice dog" smile. The dogs weren't fooled and carried on sniffing and snarling.

Andrew Kavanagh welcomed me into a barely lit hall. Light is often a problem in Borris House. I never discovered how to make the light in the lavatory work so, throughout my visit, I had to pee in the dark and hope I didn't miss. A huge Welsh dresser, spilling papers from drawers, stood against one wall. Paintings of bewigged, begowned Kavanaghs looked down.

Nothing prepared me for the glories beyond the entrance hall. Suddenly there was light. I had walked into a grand room, grand enough for dancers to waltz in. They certainly had tea dances under the blue domed ceiling. The huge windows look out on the estate.

An imposing staircase leads to the bedrooms and the library, which is much as Arthur left it. The Kavanaghs offered me tea in the vast kitchen, insisted I stay with them and, then, asked how they could help.

Later in the day, Tina Kavanagh explained they felt it was time all Arthur's papers were catalogued properly but they had never quite got round to it. Farming meant so much paperwork. She knew where some of the material was and, perhaps, I should start on that. She installed me at the table in the dining room – a table that could easily sit twenty. As I settled to read Arthur's journals – his writing was tiny – the obvious dawned on me. He sat here, talked here, lived here; he would have chosen some of the baroque china on the sideboards and bought many of the prints and paintings on the walls.

Whenever she found some new diary or document, Tina was pleased. One of the reasons for her pleasure became obvious the next day. She explained it was she who was descended from Arthur. Andrew had had to change his name when he married her. They are still immensely proud of the family history and there was no way she would have changed her name. So Andrew had to become a Kavanagh.

The biography of ...

I have been interested in Arthur Kavanagh since the early 1990s. As I started to study him, I realised I would need to go beyond the once usual conventions of academic biography for a number of reasons that will become clear.

Arthur was always both warm and wary. The reserve isn't surprising. He was born with amputations that reached beyond what doctors call "the upper third". He had small stumps where his arms and legs should have been; when he was an adult, they were about four inches long. He had no fingers and no toes. The Victorians recorded a number of such cases – and many were remarkable – like that of the painter, Sarah Biffen.

In a letter to Sir Philip Crampton, one of the grandees of Irish medicine who had been Surgeon General, Francis Boxwell admitted he had been worried during the pregnancy. Lady Harriett, Arthur's mother, had been left weak from her last childbirth. In trying to explain why the baby he had delivered had lost his limbs, the young doctor suggested a macabre process. The umbilical cord had wrapped itself round the body in the womb. Coiled like a boa constrictor round its prey, the cord had chopped off more than three-quarters of the baby's arms and legs. If the umbilical had snaked round the foetus a little higher, Arthur would have been decapitated in his mother's womb.

Explanations for birth defects were often bizarre in the 19th century. In the case of Sarah Biffen who was born near Bridgewater in Somerset, the "pixies" were said to be the cause. As odd was the explanation for Caroline Crachami, the so-called Sicilian dwarf or fairy. In 1824, Caroline Crachami fascinated London. For the hefty price of 2/6, you could visit No. 22 New Bond Street and boggle at her minuscule body; she stood just 1 foot 10 inches tall and had a squeaky voice but nice manners. According to the famous surgeon Sir Everard Home, Caroline's mother had been infected by touching a monkey – and that made her give birth to a midget. Home's fantastical theory was based on just one fact. In 1815, Madame Crachami travelled in the luggage caravan of the Duke of Wellington. During a violent storm, a monkey slipped out of its chains and ran for comfort between her legs. Madame Crachami put her hand down to scratch herself and the monkey bit her fingers. Immediately, Madame had a fit. The monkey was small and so, Home "reasoned", its bite made the foetus small. Caroline was born just seven inches tall.

Touch a monkey, look like a monkey.

Crachami died when she was nine years old, partly of exhaustion. One "viewing" at 22 New Bond Street drew over 200 people and Crachami had to talk to many of them to prove that she was not a doll but a human being.

If the monkey bite produced a midget, what would happen if a pregnant woman tripped over an elephant?

The most famous "freak" of the Victorian era was John Merrick, the Elephant Man. His doctor, Frederick Treves, told the Pathological Society of London that the patient "gave an elaborate story of a fright his mother had received shortly before the birth from being knocked down by an elephant in a circus." The encounter was enough to make Mrs Merrick give birth to a child who had a bloated skull, a deformed skeleton and flaps of grey skin, which stank.

"Cripples" and "freaks" were lucky to survive at all given the tendency the Victorians had to slaughter perfectly normal children. Crachami, Sarah Biffen, the Elephant Man and many other disabled men, women and children had to exhibit themselves to earn a living. The Elephant Man hated showing himself. He knew how ugly he looked.

Arthur Kavanagh was more fortunate. He lived to the age of 58 and he had a successful career as a landlord, traveller and politician. His family's wealth and status meant that he did not have to trade on his deformity, but he also had a steely will. Arthur never accepted there were things he should not do simply because he had no arms and no legs. He married, had children and assumed the positions expected of a man of his rank. From 1866 to 1880, he was an M.P. at Westminster.

More than a century has passed since Arthur Kavanagh left the House of Commons. I am nervous of comparing how "bad" disabilities are but I think there has never been an M.P. as disabled as Arthur was. I write this with no disrespect to contemporary politicians like David Blunkett and the wheelchair-bound Anne Begg. Arthur made no special pleas for himself other than to ask for his servant to be allowed to carry him in and out of the Chamber.

Stigma and silence

The disabled have often been under pressure to accept their fate meekly. Like blacks, Jews, women and other out-groups, the disabled mustn't grumble. I'm lucky to be alive and I'd like to thank you, Mr and Mrs Normal, for letting me walk or wheelchair down your street. I spoil the view but I won't spoil the atmosphere by reminding you that being different can sometimes be traumatic. Sorry for drawing attention to myself. Many activists complain that the disabled have been written out of history.

In English history, there were two great disabled figures before 1830 – Richard III and the poet Alexander Pope. Both Richard III and Pope could walk; both had arms and hands. Pope did not have to write with a pen held in his mouth. But both these talented men raged about their disabilities. Both had the hump – physically and psychologically – but that doesn't seem to have earned much sympathy. Of Pope, the historian J.H Plumb (1963) wrote:

> *All understanding of Pope must begin with his deformity, an ugly terrible sight which he, as much as his friends, wished to ignore but could not. Like an ineradicable dye, it stained all thought, all feelings. Deformity is commonly hideous in its effects. It corrodes character, leading to deceit, treachery, malignity and false living; and as often as not vitiates those entangled in the sufferer's life as much as the sufferer himself. So it was with Pope.*

Pope got depressed easily. He always felt people were making fun of him. He had to plot and barb to make up for his deformity. Swift sniped that Pope could not drink tea without a stratagem.

Modern psychologists would argue it was healthy for Richard III and Pope to express their anger. In his *Stigma* the American sociologist, Irving Goffman (1963) argued that if people stare at you, laugh and look away because you look so odd, sound so odd, act so odd, it hurts – and the hurt goes deep. The disabled, Goffman found, suffer depression, low self-esteem, sheer misery and "the awareness of inferiority means one is unable to keep out of consciousness the formulation of some chronic feeling of the worst sort of insecurity".

The most sympathy Plumb offers, however, is when he quotes two lines where Pope says that his soul cannot "regain its peaceful state." Instead he is doomed to

> *"How often hope, despair, resent, regret,*
> *Conceal, disdain – do all things but forget"*

Arthur Kavanagh was the opposite of Alexander Pope. Arthur hardly ever showed his feelings. In his journals, he nearly always writes as if he has no physical disability. You'd think he rides quite normally, even that he walks quite normally. In fact, he walked on his stumps only in Borris House when he was sure no one other than close friends and family would see him. You have to ferret out the rare sentence in his writings where he accepts he has no arms and legs – and even then it is usually subtle. When he was fifteen, Arthur quoted four lines of verse which reflect on "my lot" and conclude "so let me be still, and murmur not." It's very moving when you know the details of his condition. If you don't know he's limbless, it just sounds pious.

The fact that Arthur expressed so little anger, even in his private journals, suggests he taught himself to be immensely careful, immensely controlled. Psycho-suspicious today, we wonder the price people pay. Repression, depression, you need a session. Too much control just isn't normal.

Abnormal? Moi? Pull the other leg that I also don't have.

Bad taste, of course, but you could say Arthur was a control freak. I decided not to make that the title of this biography because it would be offensive but Arthur needed enormous self-control to achieve what he did.

Sources

In writing this biography I have relied largely on conventional sources – letters, archives, Arthur's journals, psychological studies, all the scholarly frills and the British and Irish press of the time, especially the rather marvellous *The Carlow Sentinel*. In 1840, on the same page of that weekly, you could find serious political comment, advice on how to get the best out of your milkers and reports of a two-headed baby born in Mongolia. Its pages give a vivid sense of Ireland during Arthur's life. Some of Lady Harriett's letters are in the archives of the National Library in Ireland – and they are a useful source. The most personal of these documents is the journal Arthur kept from when he was in his teens. It is detailed and I often quote from that. Boxwell also wrote about Arthur's progress from the very start.

The few writings on Arthur have certainly not probed the psychology of a very complex man. Arthur's cousin, Sarah Steele published a biography just after his death in 1889. Though Sarah Steele loved him and had access to documents it is now hard to trace, she focussed almost entirely on his travels. She said little about his politics. Everyone else has imitated her. In 1921, Walter Kavanagh, Arthur's eldest son, wrote a memoir after his father had died and set his career in the context of his family's history. "I only touch upon these events in Irish history to put my father in his rightful place." His rightful place is an important one. Arthur Kavanagh has every right to be seen as a hero and as a hero in disabled history. Walter did nothing to publish his memoir, however; it has languished among the family papers for 80 years.

In 1936, MacCarthy included a short chapter on Kavanagh in her book *Six Handicaps.* One of her other subjects was Beethoven – deaf but what a composer, she gushed. MacCarthy gushed less about Arthur because she often copied Steele almost verbatim and Steele was restrained like her cousin had been.

Steele is also the main source for the only two other works on Kavanagh. In 1960, *The Incredible Mr Kavanagh* told the story of Arthur's early life and of his travels in Asia. The book peters out in the 1850s, however, just as Kavanagh's political career starts. Then, in 1989, to mark the centenary of Arthur's death, Kenneth Kavanagh, published privately a short account of Arthur's life. Kenneth Kavanagh ferreted out some useful letters. Oddly, again, he also hardly deals with Arthur's political work in the last 24 years of his life when he was an M.P. and an important player in the debates about Ireland and terrorism. In 2000, an Irish historical journal carried a basic account of the facts of Kavanagh's life but added very little that is new.

There are, however, in any life, happenings and thoughts for which there is less evidence than a biographer would wish and it has become less and less exceptional to include what one might call imaginative leaps. (This mirrors the fashion in television for drama documentaries such as a recent one on the relationship between Tony Blair and Gordon Brown.)

In 1939, the then popular *London Life* ran an article about Sarah Biffen, the limbless painter who was mentioned earlier. It called her, as the Victorians did, "The Limbless Wonder". *London Life* did not stint the dramatic. The piece assumed that the paper had a reporter at the scene of Sarah's birth. And this is what the reporter witnessed allegedly, dramatically and, also, in a West country burr.

> *"Aye, thou can coom in now, Garge Biffen, it's a girl. And marcy on us, what a girl!" Said the matronly looking, poorly clad woman as she opened the door of the sleeping room, which was feebly lighted by two flickering rushlights, and admitted George Biffen, the father of the new-born child.*
>
> *"An' how be Sarah, Mary?" he asked, in the slow but not unmusical drawl of the Somersetshire rustics.*
>
> *"Finely", was the reply. "She be just a-droppin' off to sleep, so don't wake 'er, Garge."*
>
> *Garge nodded. His slow brain comprehended that sleep was his wife's best medicine.*
>
> *"An' the babby, Mary?" as a faint cry came from the bed where the woman was lying.*
>
> *"Sarah be a cuddlin' it up to her," said the woman called Mary, who was George Biffen's sister.*
>
> *"You won't blame it on her, will 'e, Garge? It baint poor Sarah's fault! When I took the baby from 'er it was a small sized un, too. I thought I'd died! Garge, it 'as no limbs. I fear the pixies 'ave lopped 'em off!"*
>
> *The yokel's slow brain found difficulty in comprehending his sister's statement.*
>
> *"No limbs?" he muttered. "D'yer mane no arms an' no legs?"*
>
> *"Yes, Garge."*
>
> *"God in 'eaven! Then 'ow can the kid work for its livin'? Mary you should have smothered it afore Sarah saw it. It be a pixie, sure enough!"*
>
> *"I thought so, too," said his trembling sister, "but I was feared, mort'ly feared! The law, Garge – the law!"*
>
> *"Feared?" said the man. "It'd be a marcy."*
>
> *"So I thought; but it 'as sich a pretty little face and, Garge, it'd be murder!"*
>
> *"Maybe so," said her brother, "but summat 'ad to be done. I'll step down to the village and ask parson wot's to do."*

This wise decision of her father saved Sarah because the vicar was not in the business of smothering infants at birth.

It is not just tabloids who use such devices. In his biography of Dickens, Peter Ackroyd included a considerable amount of fictional material. Another example comes in *Wittgenstein's Poker* by David Edmonds and John Eidinow. The book is about a heated meeting at Cambridge University's Moral Sciences Club. The philosopher of science, Karl Popper, who was then 45, was invited to address the club; Wittgenstein complained about his paper and stormed out of the room. In a detailed account of what led up to that row and how people remember it, the authors suddenly veer into "reconstruction". They imagine Wittgenstein eating a tomato sandwich on the way to the meeting, they tell us what both he and Popper were thinking before they sniped and sparred at each other and what it left them thinking later. Popper hated Wittgenstein; Wittgenstein had hardly heard of Popper. Each man wanted the approval of Bertrand Russell who was a kind of father figure to both of them. All this is imaginative, something of a leap – and quite convincing. But it is some way off from the known facts to being inside the skulls of the main actors.

I have some sympathy for both the authors of *Wittgenstein's Poker* and *London Life*'s need to imagine what happened. I have done it myself.

In 1986, in collaboration with Sara Maitland, I directed and produced a film called *Following in Vesta's Footsteps.* Sara had just written a biography of the great music hall impersonator Vesta Tilley. There were many questions Sara could not answer about her subject; Vesta Tilley had left music hall in 1918 to marry a Tory M.P. She was careful not to leave letters or documents that revealed her love life or that would explain why she never had a child. Like Arthur, Vesta was a control freak. In the film, Sara, the biographer, confronted Tilley (played by an actress) and asked all the nosey, unanswerable questions that nagged her and that she could not answer in a straightforward biography.

As a result, in a few places in this book, I have adopted this approach and embellished scenes suggested by Arthur's journals in which it seems likely he very deliberately only tells part of the story. It is important not to confuse established fact with speculation. In television, such sections are labelled "reconstruction"; I have set any such sections in italics.

How disabled children see themselves

When J.H Plumb wrote about Alexander Pope, there were virtually no studies of the psychology of disabled children. We do know more now. Between the age of four and five, children become conscious of themselves and how they are different from other people. Psychologists argue children develop a theory of "other minds". Arthur, growing up in Borris House where there were many mirrors, saw what he was like. He would have stared at the half-body in the mirror, stared at his arm stumps, stared at his leg stumps. His body wouldn't change. That was it, that was him. He was different, he was a freak of nature.

The psychology of disabled children, of how they develop and how they see themselves is a neglected field. Developmental psychology has long tried to establish the stages of which children develop – both intellectually and emotionally. Some of the most interesting work on how we develop our sense of self and of our identity is that of Eric Erikson, a not very orthodox psychoanalyst. Erikson writes about the stages of development and claims we all make choices from birth. The choices are both conscious and unconscious. A baby who is abused, for example, will be deeply affected by that. Erikson's first two key choices are

- trust versus distrust
- dependency versus autonomy

Does the baby trust the world and the people round him? Does the toddler try to explore that world and learn to master his environment or does he, or she, keep on retreating to the safety of mother, of the nanny's lap? We shall see how Arthur coped with these choices or turning points.

All the Kavanagh children: Arthur, his brothers and Hoddy.

Chapter 2

March 26 1831
Arthur's birth

Lady Harriett had not held her new baby yet. Now, some hours later, Francis Boxwell was in the nursery of Borris House with Thomas Kavanagh.

"It would be better . . . ," Dr Boxwell peered down at the cot.

"A man must finish his sentences, Hippo. What would be better?"

"If the child, if your family . . . did not have to . . . eh . . . suffer . . . this," the words finally jerked out of Boxwell's mouth. He had had little reason to suspect that this birth would be so grotesque.

"This what, Dr Boxwell?" said Thomas Kavanagh.

Boxwell couldn't bring himself to describe what lay in the cot.

"Haven't you ever seen one like this before?"

"No, Mr Kavanagh. Perhaps I'd better consult the authorities . . ."

"What fucking authorities!" Thomas Kavanagh could trace his family back to the kings of Leinster. He was used to commanding and, sometimes, surprisingly effective.

"A case like this is so rare, sir. Dr Marsh or Sir Philip Crampton, I think."

"The miracles man?"

"Sir Philip proved the cures which the Archbishop of Dublin claimed were miraculous were due to the influence of the imagination on the nerves."

"Maybe he's more interested in the truth than most doctors. You do realise I want the truth, Hippocrates?"

Dr Francis Boxwell nodded. You put up with the barkings of the aristocracy if you wanted to be paid.

"How many cases have there been where a baby grows legs after birth," asked Thomas.

"None that I know of, but that doesn't mean, sir."

"How many cases where a child grows arms after birth?"

"I've never heard of one, but that doesn't mean, sir . . ." Boxwell's voice trailed off again. He was only 28 years old. He had no idea of how to cope with this situation.

"I know my Bible, Hippocrates. A good Protestant wraps himself in the word of God. Not a single case. Not a single case in history either. I know my Shakespeare. Not a single mention of such a deformity. And don't talk of miracles."

"I didn't mention miracles, sir."

"There haven't been any in Ireland for at least 600 years." Thomas yelled for the footman standing outside the nursery. "Melrose, *The Treatise Discoursing of the Essence, Causes, Symptoms, Prognosticks and Deformities in Man and the Beasts.* Bring it from the library."

Melrose's footsteps echoed away in the corridors of Borris House. Thomas Kavanagh spoke more softly now. "How did Lady Harriett react?"

"She doesn't know. I made sure she did not see the baby. The nurse fainted."

"I'm not bloody surprised. The fucking priests will dance round the bloody altars. I can hear their sermons. God has passed judgement on the House of Kavanagh ... I will be a fucking laughing stock from Cork to Dublin."

Thomas Kavanagh kicked the two labradors nosing round the cot. He had saved Borris House when rebels surrounded it in 1798. His troop had killed fifty Fenians and, then, he tried the survivors. He was the justice of the peace but he was also just. The prisoners confessed; the priests had promised Catholics who murdered their landlords that St Peter would applaud them. Fifty-six rebels were hung.

The families of the dead cursed Thomas in 1798. Then, in 1812, an old woman cursed him after he had had her son executed. It was a country curse. It involved a withered branch on a great oak tree. One day it would sprout turnips and the House of Kavanagh would be ruled – and ruined – by a cripple.

Melrose returned with the *Treatise.* "Get out," Thomas said.

A thread of dust streamed into the air as Thomas opened the pages of the book. "Fine engravings, Hippo. Precise, anatomical, comprehensive. Dogs with two tails, cows with two heads, the half-headed boy of Lubeck, the giant of Kinsale, the Sicilian dwarf, Charles Heineken, the Danish genius who could speak Greek at three and died at four, the hermaphrodite of Uppsala." Thomas turned to the letter S. "If there had been instances, we should find them under Spontaneous. Spontaneous combustion, many examples of that. Some bodies must be packed with gunpowder. But no case, absolutely no case, of the spontaneous generation of limbs after birth."

Thomas glared at the doctor. He stopped turning the pages. "In other words you have made my wife deliver one of the most stupendous cripples in history. How will the child walk sans arms, sans legs, sans just about everything?"

"That is why we normally . . ." Boxwell was finding it hard to finish his sentences again.

"How will this child wipe his arse or hold his lance . . . at least that seems to be there . . ."

"How specific do you want me to be, sir?"

"Very specific," Thomas Kavanagh said quietly.

"A pillow usually suffices to eh . . . suffocate . . . that is quickest and they don't feel a thing, . . ."

"How do you know they don't feel a thing? Don't you swear not to harm the patient, Hippocrates?"

"Modern medicine is more realistic. The Greeks didn't even realise that the heart was a pump."

"And your conscience? This baby might grow up to be a great philosopher."

"With no arms and no legs, sir? Usually, such children are idiots as well. *Mens sana in corpore sano.* A healthy mind in a healthy body, so it follows that, in an unhealthy body, you have an unhealthy mind and, in a body amputated at birth, you have an amputated mind."

"Have you ever seen anything bloody like . . ." Now it was the father who couldn't finish his sentences.

"I have heard of one case," said Boxwell, more confident now. "There are rumours of a monster child in Glamis castle. A Strathmore."

"Is he more or less crippled than my son?"

"His condition is a mystery. The child is kept a prisoner, walled up in an isolated part of the castle . . . attended only by a valet who is also deformed."

"So the Earl of Strathmore did not kill his child."

"He had poor medical advice, sir"

Thomas poured himself a glass of port and drank it. "How often have you done it?"

"Very often, sir. Many peasants are born with deformities. Sometimes it's poor hygiene, sometimes intercourse with sheep. Often the deformed child is still born. If not, I help nature do what it always intended."

"And how much do they pay you for this murdering?"

"At least two shillings."

Thomas Kavanagh sat down. He poured himself another port and gulped it down. He made a decision that would have profound consequences. "I want to know everything about the child at Glamis. You will go there and find out. I shall expect you back by the 1st of May."

"But, sir, I have my patients here,"

"If you don't return with the answers, I shall have you arrested."

"I have committed no crime, sir."

"Dr Boxwell, the poisons you gave my poor wife while she was pregnant caused this freak of nature."

As the local justice of the peace Thomas Kavanagh could make sure that anyone found guilty would be sentenced to death. His family had been ruling Carlow for over 700 years.

The family history – damage and homage

In the 12th century, the Kavanaghs controlled the area between Carlow and Wexford. The bandit-lord Dermot MacMurrough described himself as king of Leinster. Sometimes it is impossible to precis mediaeval history without feeling it's a tale of monks and mobsters. In the Kavanagh annals, Dermot is something of a hero, a fierce warrior and a smart matchmaker; in English history, however, Dermot is one of the first unruly Celts, a hairy bandit who couldn't keep his prick in his scabbard. In 1152, Dermot kidnapped and

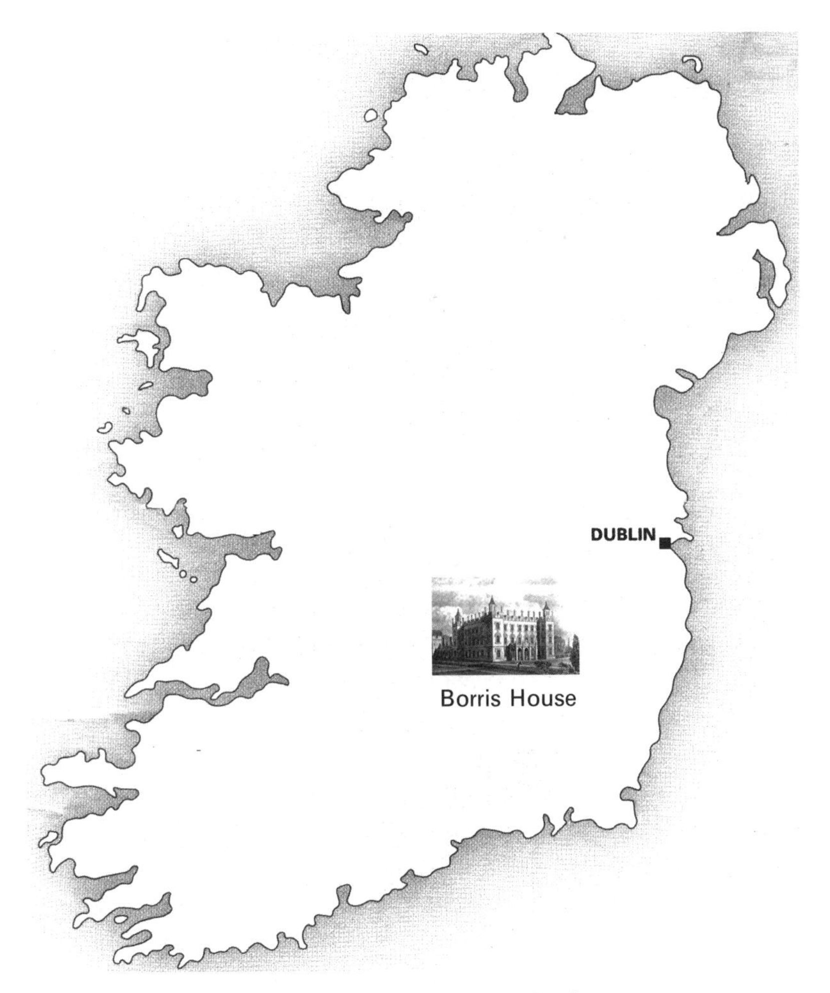

Borris House in County Carlow.

raped Dervorgil, the daughter of the King of Connacht. Connacht vowed revenge but he did nothing much about it.

In 1154, Henry II became King of England. He spent the first decade of his reign curbing the power of the barons. Ireland was not on his agenda though Henry knew the famous story of William Rufus, son of William the Conqueror. Rufus once gazed out over the Irish Sea and dreamed of ruling St Patrick's island.

In the 14 years after the rape, Dermot alienated many of his followers and quarrelled not just with Connacht, but with other local kings, like Rory of Dublin. Today, we would call him a dangerous psychopath. In 1166, Dermot needed allies and he sailed for Bristol. The city told him it could not give him any help without the permission of the King. Henry was in Bordeaux, which he also ruled as Duke of Aquitaine, so Dermot sailed again.

Henry played hard to get but being King of Ireland would be a nice bonus. He made Dermot swear homage, fealty and obedience and sent him back to England with letters patent. The letters allowed Dermot to hire any unruly barons who were ready to embark on an Irish adventure.

Dermot soon fixed a deal with two lords, Robert FitzStephen and Maurice FitzGerald. Both could muster some fighting men. As usual, though, Dermot could not bear waiting. He gathered 200 foot soldiers and sailed for Waterford. He was not much of a general. He lost the first skirmish and ended up having to pay a fine for raping and abducting Dervorgil. He was saved though when FitzStephen landed with about 400 soldiers at Waterford.

Then, the Earl of Pembroke decided to intervene on Dermot's side. Pembroke was more powerful than Fitzstephen and Fitzgerald but he wanted a guarantee in feudal triplicate that Henry allowed him to invade Ireland. Pembroke did not want the King accusing him of treason. Once he had his guarantees, Pembroke took 200 knights and 1000 foot soldiers across the Irish Sea. They landed at Wexford on August 11th. So many horsemen in such fine livery frightened the Irish, the legend goes. Waterford fell without an arrow being fired. A month later, Pembroke took Dublin but, this time, he had to fight. He proved to be an astute general and was nicknamed Strongbow.

Dermot was canny enough to cement the victory with a marriage. He married his son to Pembroke's daughter, and so his descendants became aristocrats with a place in both English and Irish history. In the National Gallery of Ireland, there is a splendid portrait of this wedding. Dermot died in 1171 and Strongbow succeeded him as King of Leinster, which was part of the marriage deal.

After Dermot's death, the Kavanagh clan flourished. In the 14th century Art MacMurrough styled himself King of Leinster. When Richard II arrived in Waterford in 1394, he hoped to subdue the pesky Art and other rebellious Irishmen. Richard brought a large army with him and, again, the Irish swore homage to the king from

London. Art Kavanagh had to give back some of the lands he had recently taken over. But he was allowed to keep most of his turf in return for acknowledging Richard's authority and a promise "to accept wages from the king to go and conquer other lands occupied by rebels against the king". Richard even knighted Art. The King of Leinster soon regretted doing homage, however, and sent Richard a letter saying he would never bend the knee again. Shakespeare gave the defiant Art a brief mention in Richard II as "a puissant lord".

It was not till 1541 that the Kavanaghs stopped styling themselves as Kings of Leinster and became loyal subjects of the Crown. The first visit of a Kavanagh to London took place in 1613 when Morgan Kavanagh became an M.P. He sat for only two years, however.

When Cromwell ransacked Ireland, Morgan's son was wily enough not to have his lands confiscated even though the family was Catholic. The Kavanaghs remained Catholic after the accession of William and Mary in 1688. In the 18th century, one Kavanagh became the British minister in Prague. Another rose to be the chamberlain to Maria Theresa who ruled the Austro-Hungarian Empire. There were revolutionary Kavanaghs too; one Joseph Kavanagh was at the front of the crowd who stormed the Bastille in 1789 though we don't know much else about him.

By the time Arthur's father, Thomas Kavanagh was born in 1767, the family was one of the richest in Ireland. Their estates were huge.

Thomas was brought up as a Catholic and no one seems sure why he converted to being a Protestant. He sat in the Irish Parliament in 1796 for County Carlow.

Thomas was a sharp and self-confident man. When the Wolfe Tone uprising started in 1798, he sent the great family heirlooms, the iron crown of Leinster and the charter horn of Leinster to Trinity College, Dublin for safekeeping. It was wise. Five thousand peasants and priests besieged Borris House and Thomas was lucky to rout them.

The 1798 revolt changed the relationship between England and Ireland. With its own Parliament, Ireland was too much like an independent kingdom. In 1801, the Act of Union dissolved the Irish Parliament. From then on Irish members sat at Westminster but Thomas did not seek election to the House of Commons. He didn't like London.

Thomas married Lady Elisabeth Butler in 1799. She was the daughter of the Earl of Ormonde, an old Irish Protestant family. When his wife died in 1822, Thomas had no intention of remaining single. Only one of his sons was still alive; the other two had died very young. Thomas started looking for a suitable wife – a woman young enough to give him many more sons. He found Harriett Le Poer Trench.

Lady Harriett came from a Huguenot family who had fled France after the St Bartholomew massacre. Her father, the Earl of Clancarty was a good friend of the Duke of Wellington who made him one of the English ambassadors to the Congress of Vienna. After Napoleon's defeat at the Battle of Waterloo in 1815, the Congress settled the boundaries of Europe. Talleyrand wrote that the Earl of Clancarty was a talented negotiator and an honourable man.

The Earl was very fond of his daughter and Harriett sometimes travelled with him. As a fifteen-year-old, she danced at the ball held on the eve of the Battle of Waterloo. Seven years later, however, she was still unmarried and she had a habit of annoying suitors with her all too definite opinions. Such a plain woman should be more pliable. Harriett was surprisingly sure of herself, of her faith and of her opinions.

Thomas Kavanagh did not impress Harriett but she agreed to marry him. The local people thought her haughty, unpleasant and, even, evil. The truth was that Harriett missed the glamour of Europe. After Brussels, Borris was very dull. She insisted that her husband stand for Parliament because they would have to spend some time in London. Thomas wanted to please his new wife so in 1826, he went back to the Commons.

Harriett had three children before Arthur. After seeing his deformed body, she decided not to sleep with Thomas ever again but, for once, she was shrewd enough not to announce her decision or to justify it with Biblical quotations. Thomas lived in hope that their marital relations would resume. Meanwhile, the frustration made it harder for him to control his temper. His children and his tenants would suffer for that. Arthur was born to these not very well-matched parents.

Sarah Biffen

As he looked for guidance, Boxwell learned about the fate of Sarah Biffen who, like Arthur, had no arms or legs. By 1831 she was quite famous. Just after her birth, the local vicar visited her and agreed to baptise her. He gave strict instructions that she was to be treated as a crippled child, not some freak of nature. This was important because many of the local folk said she was a "pixie" birth. Sarah did not grow up in a fine house like Arthur but in a poor and, according to *London Life*, "squalid" farm labourer's cottage. But she showed remarkable intelligence at an early age. She soon learned to roll and trundle herself about. She could pick up things with her mouth, and was, in all respects, normal, apart from the fact that she was armless and legless.

Just as Boxwell had supposed Arthur might be mentally defective, the local villagers believed Sarah had to be an idiot. When it became obvious she was anything but she became a local celebrity, and her parents sometimes charged people to come and gawp at her.

The vicar of East Quantoxhead, near Bridgewater, where Sarah was born, taught her to read; and, then, Sarah taught herself to write by holding a pencil in her mouth and copying words on paper. By the time she was seven, Sarah could read and write well which was exceptional for a "normal" West country farm labourer's daughter. She used to be carried and wheeled in a barrow by her mother. Her father liked to drink and sometimes his daughter came with him to the local inn. Sometimes at night when a paper arrived from Bath or Bristol, she would read the news "to the yokels of the execution of Marie Antoinette and other tragedies and events of the French Revolution."

The vicar clearly thought Sarah something of a miracle. He placed the books in the rectory library at her disposal. She read them avidly. Then, she started to copy engravings and woodcuts and, thanks to her *aptitude* for taking infinite pains, was soon able to draw and sketch. When she was 12, Sarah reached the height of 37 inches: she never grew taller. She was, therefore, slightly larger than Arthur.

Then, Sarah's life changed forever. A Mr Dukes came one day to Quantoxhead and watched Sarah write and draw. He was amazed and went to find her father, George Biffen. He bought George a large amount of alcohol and eventually pressed a 5 Pound note into his hand. This was the price of his daughter. Sarah then agreed to bind herself to Mr Dukes for sixteen years, in return for 5 Pounds per annum. Dukes had an eye for a good deal. He would pay "for all necessaries and provide what she required to keep her in health and decency." But in return he would be able to show her at a profit.

In practice, Sarah became Dukes' slave. He took her all over the country from fair to fair, where she was exhibited as "The Limbless Wonder" in a booth. Depending on the venue, the public would be charged from 3d. to 1/– for admission.

And Sarah performed. Perched upon a pedestal, with a kind of easel beside her, Sarah used to write her autograph for a penny, and write letters at dictation from 3d. each, depending on how long they were. She would also draw crayon portraits, and paint little landscapes.

Dukes made a great deal of money by exhibiting Sarah whom he overworked shamefully; he even compelled her to paint landscapes and portraits of celebrities on Sundays. This went on until, at the age of 28, Sarah's sixteen years of servitude ended.

In 1812 at Swaffham, Sarah Biffen finally enjoyed a major piece of luck. A certain Lord Morton and some friends paid their shillings and entered the booth to see Sarah paint miniature portraits with brush and pen held in her mouth. The portraits were sold for 2 to 3 guineas.

Lord Morton was amazed at her artistic ability, started to talk with her and heard her life story. As her contract with Dukes was on the point of expiring, Morton took her away and arranged for her further art training by a famous portrait painter and illustrator of the period, Craig. Sarah progressed rapidly. Several exhibitions of her works followed, and her water colours fetched high prices.

Both George IV and William IV visited the exhibitions and purchased her pictures.

Eventually in 1821, Sarah was awarded the Gold Medal of the Society of Arts, and commissions started to pour in. She developed the skill of painting miniature portraits on ivory which was hugely fashionable at the time.

By the time Boxwell started to make inquiries, he was convinced that Arthur was not condemned to a useless life. And what he saw at Glamis only made him more convinced of that.

The monster of Glamis, April 1831

Thomas Kavanagh had hoped some miracle might occur but when Boxwell returned from Glamis, Arthur was exactly the same. "No spontaneous generation, you see," he snorted at Boxwell.

"What did you find out? What is the monster of Glamis like?"

"I had to bribe the servants to see him. He is pitiful. He has a hunch and his face is bloated. There is half a bucket of water inside his skull."

"So he'd be better off dead."

"I am afraid so, sir."

"I am not a coward. I'll watch while you kill my son."

"May I just perform a few experiments, sir?"

Thomas Kavanagh was surprised but he agreed. Boxwell felt the stump of each of the baby's legs. He held each stump a few seconds and, then, let it fall on the cot.

Then, Boxwell clapped his hands behind the baby. The baby's reactions surprised him. He turned round, startled. Boxwell's next experiment was simple. He started to tickle the baby's stomach. And then he poked his tongue out at Arthur. Boxwell was amazed to see the baby was poking his tongue back at him.

"Your son's reactions are normal, it's just as I feared," Boxwell said. He looked up from the cot and faced Thomas. "Sir, what the Strathmores have done to Thomas is monstrous. The boy smashes his head against walls whenever he sees himself in the mirror. He is to be pitied."

"He has arms and legs – more than this poor wretch" Thomas sighed. "You need a pillow, I presume," he added

Boxwell hesitated. "I am no longer sure, sir."

"Sure you know how to kill a baby? I thought you had considerable experience of that."

"Of what to recommend, sir. Thomas..I will not call him the monster, is not just deformed but an imbecile. Your son has a good face. His reactions are those of an alert baby, not an idiot, as I assumed when he was born. Let's see if he can follow this."

Boxwell took out a feather and moved it from right to left. Almost on cue, Arthur's eyes followed.

"Now let us try this," Boxwell moved the feather up and down now.

"The child sees and responds normally. When I landed in Dublin, sir, I visited Sir Philip Crampton. He believes he may be able to construct artificial legs so that your son could walk."

"Like a mechanical man?"

"And then, sir, there is Lady Harriett. I would have told her the baby had died of complications. She had never seen the child. She could not love a baby she had not seen. Now she has a mother's feelings."

Lady Harriett was delighted to learn of Boxwell's experiments. She praised her husband for being so brave that he would not permit their son to be smothered to death.

She put her hand on her husband's arm. "I have arranged for Dr Boxwell to talk to the servants, Thomas. The doctor can explain the medical condition better than you or I could. Dr Boxwell tells me Sir Philip Crampton has written about our son to the great Dr Edgeworth who knows more about the education of cripples than anyone."

"I just don't want anyone fucking saying the curse of Kavanagh has come true," Thomas Kavanagh said, "I'll kill them if they do."

Boxwell's inspiring address to the Kavanagh servants, May 1831

Boxwell had been shocked by the fate of "the monster of Glamis". He had no intention of making another child suffer in the same way. So Boxwell became an advocate of the power of positive thinking even though, of course, the concept hadn't been invented then. He encouraged Harriett and Thomas to give the baby a name that reflected the most glorious episodes in the family past. The infant was christened Arthur MacMurrough after the "puissant lord" who had defied Richard II. Boxwell explained to Lady Harriett and her husband that the servants had to understand his approach; everything depended on how they behaved towards Arthur.

The only text of his speech we have comes from a letter Boxwell wrote to Sir Philip Crampton. Boxwell started by confronting the legend of the curse of the Kavanaghs. In modern times, he laughed, people did not believe in curses any more than they believed in trolls and fairies. Then, he turned to the heart of the matter. He told the staff:

> *You need to behave as if the child was normal, to set the normal challenges of childhood. You must not cosset the child. You must make him unaware of fear from the cradle. It may seem cruel to appear indifferent, to ignore his screams and not to let him feel dependent on you but, in the end, it will be an immense kindness. If he has no fears, he will not hesitate to take risks and risks he must eventually take if he is to become as other children.*

Boxwell added that he "believed the boy would make good and confound them although at the time I hardly dared accept my own optimism." In modern terms, Boxwell insisted they must not make the child too dependent. You could argue he was an early advocate of what we know in psychology as learned helplessness theory (Seligman 1968). Seligman claims that feeling helpless and defeated leads to depression. Both rats who cannot do anything to escape from electric shocks and human beings who feel trapped in their situations, tend to become seriously depressed. The reverse is also true. If someone who is depressed can un-learn old habits and reject the "I can't do anything to improve my lot" defeatism, their mental health tends to improve.

A hundred and forty years before Seligman proposed his theory of learned helplessness, Boxwell acted on something like it. By mastering his body and his environment, Arthur would overcome.

Arthur also had a duty to history, a duty to the glorious, puissant ancestors. "Above all," Boxwell told the servants at Borris, "he must be made conscious of his heritage and instilled with a sense of destiny. He must feel in his bones that he has a mission to fulfil for this is the only way in which he will overcome his grievous handicap. But again he is fortunate in having a family who by their manifold examples can point the way for him."

The servants clapped – and they were right to. It was an inspiring speech. And so Arthur Kavanagh didn't just live but he became a living experiment. Could a baby who was so disabled thrive? Could he become a normal boy who could laugh, bully, make friends and tear the wings off butterflies?

Thomas and Lady Harriett decided, however, that Tom, Charley and Harriett, Arthur's brothers and sisters, would not be told the truth. They were too young to understand. It would be too traumatic. They needed time.

Boxwell also had some sense of the pressure on the parents. He encouraged them, told them how brave they were being to keep them well motivated. After visiting the famous Dr Marsh and Sir Philip Crampton, Boxwell wrote to Lady Harriett; "You have displayed wondrous patience and cheerfulness over all this and I never cease to marvel at it. Our joint task must be to make him entirely unconscious of his limitations or his disabilities, as far as is humanly possible."

The joint task meant the two of them would have to spend a great deal of time together supervising Arthur – and they both seemed pleased by the prospect.

Chapter 3

A lack of experts

By 1831, there were plenty of books giving parents advice on how to bring up their children well. In her book *Perfect Parents* (1995) Hardyment traces how-to-be-a-mother-and-father books back to the 16th century. But none of these handbooks mentioned profoundly disabled children.

Francis Boxwell had made his speech on instinct. Inspiring the staff and parents turned out to be easier than getting any useful information. Boxwell praised Dublin's great medical authorities like Sir Philip Crampton and Marsh when he was speaking to Lady Harriett but they were surgeons. They were intrigued by the possibility of machine imitating man, of designing artificial legs, which could bend at the knee. At the same time, there were new metal-working techniques. A firm in York specialised in making the most modern limbs. Crampton and Marsh were keen to help especially as the Kavanaghs could afford to pay for the best new artificial leg for little Arthur.

When Boxwell asked specific questions about how to educate so disabled a child, however, Crampton admitted he didn't know much. Edgeworth turned out to be an expert on midwifery. In Trinity College Library Boxwell found that texts on how to educate disabled children were not plentiful. Ancient tomes like *The Lives of the Saints* referred to infants who had been born deaf, blind or deformed, like the mediaeval Gilbert of Sempringham. Gilbert was born a hunchback and his family abused him. His father mocked him so cruelly that Gilbert stopped speaking but the boy had the ultimate teacher. God was with him. So Gilbert blossomed, started talking again, did his miracles and got sainted. Miracle stories, Boxwell complained,

One of the few writers to even touch on the education of the disabled in the early 19th century: Heinrich Pestalozzi (1746–1827) and his son.

were not much help in suggesting how to teach Arthur the most basic skills.

Less pious texts were not much more useful. They were crammed with philosophical speculation rather than practical advice. Even the most progressive writers on education ignored disabled children.

Heinrich Pestalozzi (1746–1827) set up two interesting social experiments where poor children got formal teaching while working on farms. Literate peasants were his aim. Pestalozzi's *A Book for the People* appeared in 1824 in England and his *Letters on Early Education* in 1827. Pestalozzi said much about the education of deaf mutes but little about how to help physically disabled children. Pestalozzi came close to arguing they didn't deserve to live. If their mothers killed them, they were weak rather than wicked; it was natural, a kind of "self-defence". Pestalozzi made Boxwell wonder if he had been wrong not to smother Arthur, wrong to talk Thomas Kavanagh out of it. But he didn't wonder long. When he looked at Arthur, Boxwell was absolutely sure he had done the right thing.

The wild boy of Aveyron

In 1831, there was an account of the education of one disabled child – the wild boy of Aveyron. He was brought to Paris, and examined by Philip Pinel, the "father" of psychiatry who declared him feeble-minded. The wild boy was then handed over to a young French doctor, Jean Marc Itard. But the wild boy's problem was that he had lived with wolves and that he couldn't talk. Itard spent years teaching him to make a few grunts and to use a fork. The case was much discussed throughout Europe. Harlan Lee (1975) has looked at the controversies surrounding the wild boy and how they helped create a completely new interest in the education of the deaf and the mentally handicapped.

In the 1830s, Crampton sniped that Itard had worked no miracles but Arthur and the wild boy were utterly different. Growing up at Borris was hardly living with wolves.

The only author to offer anything was one of Pestalozzi's pupils, Froebel (1782–1852) who was aware, at least, of the need to educate mentally handicapped children. But he too was silent on the subject of the physically disabled.

Boxwell was depressed by the absence of precedents. But Lady Harriett looked up to him; he had to appear confident, as if he did have a method. There were practical matters to attend to. Lady

Harriett consulted him on whom to hire to look after Arthur. She had been recommended a wet nurse who lived in Dublin. She took Boxwell to meet Anne Fleming.

Boxwell liked her. Anne had considerable experience and she understood his ideas. Best, she found Arthur to be a very sweet baby. His appearance didn't bother her. Boxwell insisted it would damage the baby if Anne felt too sorry and frightened for Arthur. She had to give him just as much stimulation as if he were normal. When she played with him, she mustn't make allowances out of pity.

Usually, servants who looked after the children of the aristocracy saw the mother and father of their charges fairly rarely. Thomas Kavanagh hardly ever looked in on his son; he had had little to do with his other children. But Lady Harriett often visited the nursery. Dr Boxwell came virtually every day to check on the baby. Making Arthur normal was their project.

The violinist who had no arms

Arthur Kavanagh and Sarah Biffen were far from being the only disabled Victorians to achieve the heroic. Edgar Unthan was a proud, wilful Hungarian whose son was born with normal legs but with no arms. Unthan had three rules for his baby son. To show the child no pity, to be enormously patient and to help him find ways that made it possible for him to perform "normal" behaviours.

Unthan was trained to bend his legs and toes so till they became astonishingly supple. In his autobiography, he describes how he first learned to wash his face, using his toes to pick up the washcloth. He was then supple enough to bend his legs to mop his face. No one would ever have heard of Unthan if he hadn't gone on to develop a far more remarkable skill – playing the violin with his feet. He became a virtuoso violinist whose concerts were admired both by audiences and critics. His Beethoven was particularly moving as the public loved hearing the deaf composer played by the armless violinist!

Arthur's parents could also look to Sarah Biffen for inspiration. As she grew older Sarah Biffen attracted the attention of Queen

Typing with no arms.
C.H. Unthan called his biography "The Armless Fiddler: A Pediscript". (One has to wonder with no disrespect why he didn't call it "A Footnote".)

Victoria, who always took a great interest in out-of-the-ordinary people. Victoria had become a patron of Isaac Van Ambergh, the lion tamer (1800–1858) who was the first man to put his head in a lion's mouth as part of his act and a patron of "Tom Thumb". As soon as she heard that "Miss Biffen", the fashionable miniature painter, was a limbless freak, Queen Victoria summoned her. Then, she commissioned Sarah to paint miniature portraits of the late King Edward and his sister.

Sarah Biffen died in 1850 and some of her work can be found today in the royal galleries at Windsor Castle.

Borris House: May 1 1831

Only Arthur's parents and Dr Boxwell could walk into the nursery. The others had to knock first and wait until Arthur's nurse said they could come in. If the baby was at the breast, she told them to wait. Arthur always howled if he had the nipple snatched away. It was a very deliberate plan to make sure that Arthur's brothers and sister did not rush in and see how disabled their brother was.

But it is not easy to keep things from children. When Arthur was 3 months old his siblings came to see him in the nursery. They liked Anne and they were carrying a huge bunch of yellow flowers.

But there was no vase in the room. She was, for once, careless. Arthur was sleeping. She told them to be very quiet and not disturb their baby brother. Then, she left the children alone for a few minutes while she went to get a vase.

Arthur was wrapped up in what he later referred to as "his sack." It covered his torso and the tiny stumps of both his arms and legs. There were sleeves and legs at each of the four ends, which were tied in a pretty bow – blue for a boy. He looked more like a box of chocolates than a baby.

While Anne was gone, it seems that Tom, the eldest boy who was six, decided to tickle the baby. He started with the baby's toes. But he soon discovered that where there should be toes, there was nothing. Feeling nothing, Tom began patting up the leg of the sack. There was nothing. He patted the cloth more carefully, searching for an answer. But there was more sack than baby.

Finally, he touched it. Arthur's stump.

Tom yelled in amazement that Arthur did not seem to have a leg. He wanted the others to confirm that but Charley would not. He was always rather timid.

Tom then checked the other leg. Again, he was baffled. This baby seemed to be legless. Near Arthur's groin Tom found flesh again.

Tom wanted to see, to find an explanation. Slowly, as if something were going to bite him, Tom pulled back the left sleeve. Then he saw the truth. The stump, the knobbly flesh, the funny folds of skin.

Nothing would stop Tom now. He unpeeled the left arm of the sack. He pulled the right and left sleeves up. He looked down and gasped at his baby brother. No arms, no legs, no hands, no feet, no fingers, no toes.

No toenails, no fingernails either.

No one had ever seen a human being missing so much.

Tom was so amazed he did not hear Anne coming back.

Casually, she walked into the nursery with the daffodils in a vase. When he realised that, Tom tried desperately to stick Arthur back into his sack. He was too late, too flustered, too clumsy. Anne saw what he had done; she was livid. She picked up the baby she was already starting to love. "You must never do that again. I don't want to see you here again." She told the children that they had to find their mother and confess what they had done. She locked the door after them.

The commotion had woken Arthur. She gave him her nipple to calm him down.

A few minutes later, a hard knock at the door. "I do not expect the nursery to be locked, Anne," Lady Harriett said angrily.

Anne took the baby from the breast at once. She buttoned her dress and ran to open the door. Dropped back in the cot, taken off the nipple, Arthur howled.

"I will not have you locking the door, Anne." Lady Harriett then rounded on her children and said she was very ashamed of them. She insisted they apologise to Arthur. The children complied. Then, Lady Harriett undid the bows of all the sleeves. She took off all Arthur's clothes.

"That is what God has given us, boys."

"Yes, Mama," Tom said.

"We must accept the works of the Lord."

"Yes, Mama,"

"You will kiss your brother ... on his arms and legs."

"But he doesn't have any," Tom pointed out.

"On his stumps. That is the word, stump."

"But Mama."

Lady Harriett smacked Tom very hard. He burst into tears. Charley trembled. Seeing that, his mother told him to come to her and then hit him across the face. He cried too. "You will do what you are told," Lady Harriett said.

Tom bent down. He held Arthur's left leg stump in his hand. His face was tight with terror. Tom was made to kiss the stump. Lady Harriett then turned to Charley.

"You too, Charley. God sends us cripples for a purpose. They allow us to show how good we are. Kiss your brother's stump."

"If we kiss it enough might we make it grow," Tom asked.

"That's the kind of superstitious nonsense peasants believe in this country. Arthur will never have arms and never have legs. He's just got to make the best of it. God must have wanted it this way and we can't hope to understand God's mind. You can go now, boys, but I expect you to pray for forgiveness tonight."

Lady Harriett told her two able-bodied sons to leave.

"I thought you'd have more sense than to leave him alone with them, Anne. If anything like it happens again, you will be dismissed."

"I am very sorry, my Lady."

"He's got such a beautiful face. It's such a pity."

Piaget and Kavanagh

There are descriptions of Anne playing with Arthur when he was six and nine months old. By then he was developing well. Boxwell taught Anne that she must encourage Arthur to use his arm and leg stumps to feel objects and toys. On this point, the surgeon Crampton gave good advice. Arthur had to develop as much power as he could in his little stumps. The more he used them, the more skilful they would become.

Boxwell had hit on an approach that would have earned the approval of Jean Piaget (1896–1980), the most influential child psychologist of the 20th century.

The newborn baby was all confusion, Piaget said. He often compared babies to primitive savages who didn't have the most basic awareness, the awareness of being a separate creature, the awareness that "I" exist and am not "you". Piaget wrote "the baby is submerged in a chaos of interesting impressions without there being any distinction between his internal state and things outside" (1952).

Eye–hand co-ordination was the root of all intelligence, Piaget believed and one's eye has to make sense of all the parts of one's body it sees. The baby "looks at his own body the way we look at a strange animal," Piaget noted. As an adult I know I will my hand to move to pick up that tasty apple, I know my hand is linked to my body and I can anticipate the apple's crunchy taste. I also know I have a separate body and that at the end of my toes there is the rest of the world.

But the newborn doesn't realise, Piaget claimed, that his hand is part of his body – let alone that he can will his hand to move. The baby doesn't connect the image of the hand with the movements he sees.

In his theory, Piaget called the first stage of development the sensorimotor stage – as the name suggests, motor movements are crucial. The child learns to link touch and vision. Two processes start working in the first months of life – **assimilation** and **accommodation**. Piaget said that we assimilate information all the time. Sounds, sights, smells, touch sensations deluge us but the brain can only cope with so much by filtering some of it out. **Accommodation** is more than filtering out, however. For Piaget, accommodation occurs when "the environment acts on the organism" and, as a result, the organism has to re-adjust and re-organise itself.

This perpetual stream and yo-yo – the baby is deluged with impressions and information, the brain filters, the brain responds, the brain changes so that it reacts differently to the next cascade of information – produces "schemas" as Piaget called them. Schemas are our first mental representations.

This is a complicated idea, best illustrated. A baby touches a ring suspended above its cot. The baby makes the ring swing back and forth, then holds it and, then, sucks it. The child's ideas or schemas about grasping, seeing, touching are changed by these new experiences; the baby learns this particular ring belongs to the class of objects that also can be sucked and touched. The baby also learns ring-like objects feel and taste different from bottles, say – an important fact of life.

The sight and feel of the ring are assimilated which leads to a change or accommodation of the concept of rings.

When Piaget started, with his wife's help, to observe their children he quickly saw the progress they made. When his daughter Jacqueline was two weeks old, Piaget found that, if he placed his finger against her cheek, she turned her head and opened her little mouth – as if to take the nipple. At 23 days, his son, Laurent would search for the nipple with his mouth. If the nipple touched his right cheek, he would turn to the right to look for it.

Piaget reckoned both these actions were first signs of searching, "searchings which prolong reflex activity and which are as yet devoid of intention." The baby didn't will them but they were still the first step to intentional and intelligent behaviour. By the time they were 3 months old, Piaget's babies were far more active and co-ordinated. They would react to noises by turning in the right direction. They would look at objects. They would reach out for them. The use of the hands now became crucial.

One of the key differences between apes and us is that we soon learn to point to objects. Later, the toddler points and says "what's that?" or calls "that's a car, a horse, a bed." Pointing with our hands is part of learning that sounds – and then words – stand for objects.

Piaget also argued that one of the ways in which small babies learn is by dropping objects. The baby lets a ball drop from its grasp, for example. Where's the bright thing gone then? Mummy or Daddy picks it up. "Here it is, baby." Then baby grabs for it, feels it, drops it again. Manipulation makes us human and intelligent.

But how does a child with no hands or arms manage this? What happens when there is no hand for the eye to co-ordinate with?

As a small baby, Arthur was already starting to compensate for his lack of hands. He used the end of his stumps as much as possible. He couldn't grasp things but he could touch and feel objects like any other baby. Anne often held out toys for him; he had to crawl towards her to get them. Sometimes, she even teased him. Arthur learned how to sit up normally and he was crawling by the time he was nine months old.

Boxwell had no idea whether the boy would try to walk. He was amazed when the 18 month-old Arthur started to pull himself up on his stumps. Thomas Kavanagh and Lady Harriett now encouraged her three older children to visit their new brother and to play with him. They all admired him as he started to learn to balance and lurched his first steps on his tiny stumps. They had grown somewhat and were now about three inches long. It was time, Boxwell and Lady Harriett decided, to see if they could fit him into artificial legs.

Earlier, it was argued that at some points it may be helpful to include what television would call reconstructions. The first concerns sugar tongs. When he was 1 year old Arthur was not, of course, keeping a diary which is why this is what I propose to call an 'imaginative leap'.

Arthur's diary: the sugar tongs incident August 1832

Dr Boxwell visits me often in the nursery.

"This is a soldier," Dr Boxwell holds it out for me to see.

"The toys don't do justice to the uniforms. Soldiers are so dashing," my mother smiles.

I can't pick the soldier up, of course, so I'm left looking the puking, pathetic infant as usual. My mother takes me in her arms and kisses me. She holds me against the swell of her breasts. She smells very different from Anne, a clean smell of sunlight and lavender.

"Poor child . . . maybe Thomas was too kind not to let you . . ." My mother does not finish her sentence.

"I'm sure you made the right decision," Boxwell reassures her.

"We don't even know if he's an imbecile," my mother pets my head.

"He's no imbecile," Anne holds one of the soldiers under my nose, smiles, "It's Wellington."

"Wellington did not look like that," my mother rebukes. "I did dance at the ball before the battle of Waterloo."

"I am sorry, my Lady," Anne says.

I want to hold the toy between my fingers like my ten toed ten fingered brothers and sisters. I can't possibly do it. The only thing I can do is grab the toy soldier in my mouth like rock candy.

"Some tea, Ma'am," the new under parlour maid arrives and is told to pour. The girl looks down at the tray, the sugar, the cup. Then, she reaches for an implement I have never seen before – a silver object with two long arms. Bringing these arms together at the tip, the girl picks up a lump of sugar.

The silver object holds the sugar lump, which the maid drops into my mother's tea. Now, she looks up. She sees me as I am. She stares, shrieks and spills the tea. It splashes on the carpet, over the front of my mother's dress.

"Can't you even manage sugar tongs, you stupid child," my mother snaps.

"Very sorry, Ma'am."

"You will pick up your things, take a week's wages and leave this house. You're too clumsy."

The girl bursts into tears. Boxwell says nothing. My mother summons other servants to mop up her floor, her dress, her jewels. But in the flurry, I just look at the silver object. So they were called tongs. I want to inspect them minutely. They could hold anything that wasn't too wide – toy soldiers, sweets, bits of food.

"I really see no reason not to have you thrashed," my mother tells the under parlour maid.

"But, my Lady."

Neither Anne nor Dr Boxwell dare say a word.

To my amazement, a word forms on my lips. I have never said a word before. I am, after all, just 15 months old.

"Tongs," I say.

Everyone stares at me. They peer down at my lips.

"Did I hear Arthur speak?" It's my mother, amazed, delighted.

"Tongs, tongs, tongs," I la-la.

"I think he said tongue, Lady Harriett," Dr Boxwell confirms.

"He likes his food," says Anne.

I mean tong – not tongue – and would explain if I could speak or spell.

"We must have imagined it," says Boxwell, "the first word a child utters is usually ma or pa".

"Did little Arthur say tongue," coos Anne.

"It is certainly young to speak. Hoddy, Tom and Charley didn't utter a word till much later. It suggests my Arthur is not an imbecile," my proud mother glows. She turns to the under parlour maid. "I may give you another chance. Seeing Arthur is a bit of a shock the first time."

Everyone agrees that, though I have a sweet face, I am a bit of a shock, I can cause the unwary to faint, shriek or shit in their pants. They don't, of course, use the last word but it's what they mean.

But my mother smiles. Her son is a verbal virtuoso.

I feel inspired. I will learn to use my stumps like the sugar tongs. I will exercise them, they will get stronger and more flexible. One day I'll be able to bring my left and my right stumps together. Then I'll be able to hold toy Wellingtons, toy Nelsons, toy soldiers or anything else – and my mother will keep on smiling and petting me.

That night in my cot, I try to force the left and the right stump to touch. I can't do it. But I won't give up. Skin, bone and sinew can stretch and grow. Every night I try and try and try again.

It became second nature for the rest of my life. Pathetic as they were, my stumps did grow a little. Later, I persuaded Anne to measure them regularly. In my mind I thumped tables in triumph every time the stumps were a fraction of an inch longer.

"How long do you think they'll be when I'm a man?" I ask Anne when I'm four.

"You poor little boy," Anne sobs.

"Don't cry," I say. I tell myself it is a practical question. If my stumps grow to 4 inches long and I strain them together, one day I may be able to pick up a spoon. And then I'll be a man.

"You'll never grow arms or legs, Mr Arthur," Anne cuddles me. There's no point in telling her my plan. She'll start talking about it to all Borris and then people will laugh at me if I fail. Or they'll be kind to the cripple who tries so hard which would be even worse.

But I know I'll surprise them and I know how happy that will make my mother.

"*Magic moments*"

The most basic human form, the stick insect man, has a body, head, arms and legs. Psychologists like Seymour Fisher (1983) have devoted their careers to studying body image and its distortions. Individuals who worry their body image is ugly or abnormal often get depressed and, sometimes, try to change they way they look.

We have seen that Piaget wondered what babies thought they saw when they looked at their own bodies. Children soon learn what looks normal, what's pretty and ugly in the eyes of others. Normal infants can recognise themselves in the mirror by the time they are 21 to 24 months old. Some evidence suggests other species can do that too, especially chimps. But even if the monkey does recognise that he is the monkey in the mirror, it doesn't seem to mean such. As far as we know, no ape worries about whether they look nicely turned out in the mirror, the kind of chimp the girls will fall for. But human beings judge what we see in the mirror when we look at ourselves – and it often makes us anxious and unhappy. Bull (1981) has studied facial disfigurement and the misery it causes. Why should having a deformed body feel any different?

Borris House was full of mirrors and full of children. Arthur could not escape seeing how he looked and how different he looked from the rest of the world. Before he was three, inevitably, he realised he was different, damaged.

Disabled children can be clever, stupid, outgoing, neurotic, extraverted, psychotic, well adjusted just like ordinary children but the reality of the missing limbs is there like a given. It can't be changed. That's me with the tiny fingers sprouting from my shoulders. I can learn to use them to write or mop my face or brush my teeth but that's how I look and no plastic surgery can do anything about that kind of disability. Research on thalidomide children showed they often felt depressed.

In *The Mental and Emotional Development of the Thalidomide Children and the Psychological Reactions of the Mothers: A Follow-Up Study* Gouin-Decarie, Ph.D of the Rehabilitation Institute of Montreal interviewed mothers of 20 thalidomide children and tested the infants themselves. She compared the IQ scores obtained during the first evaluation (1964) and those obtained at the time of follow-up (1966). Though the children had been perceived as subnormal at first, just as Boxwell had assumed Arthur was, the study showed a clear increase in IQ scores from a low of 88 to an average of 98.

The children were tested on four main factors: locomotor ability, personal–social relationships, language, and adaptive behaviour to objects. At first, and very surprisingly, it seemed the infants performed best in the area of fine motor coordination and least well in language. The second evaluation showed progress in speech development but far worse motor co-ordination problems.

Using techniques based on Piaget's work, the Canadian researchers found that about 80 percent of the infants in the sample were slower than the average child in acquiring fundamental spatial notions. They had a reasonable sense of proximity, the most primitive of all relationships, but they did not have a good sense of projective space. When they moved, they found it hard to coordinate the change in their point of view. They also relied very little on touch.

Ethel Roskies, of the Institute, interviewed mothers at length and found no simple, direct correlation between the nature and severity of the handicap and the mother's judgement of the child's normality or abnormality, her feelings about the child, or how it affected the way they handled the children. The children themselves revealed no simple relationship between level of handicap and general level of development. The mother's perception of her limb-deformed or limb-missing child is a very complex mix of psychological and sociological factors – and it changes through time. With only one exception, all the mothers spontaneously expressed the wish their child had died at the time of birth. "This phenomenon is so universal in our sample as to be considered part of the normal reaction pattern in the case of a limb-deficient child," the researchers said. Lady Harriett would clearly have felt that – and it explains some of her subsequent behaviour.

The great hope by the 1960s when the thalidomide study was done, was prostheses. Any stumps or "deformed appendages" were viewed as useless, and experts hoped that clever prostheses would help the children.

Slowly, the mothers started to accept that their babies would neither die nor be miraculously cured, but would continue to live and to cope as best they could. But as much in the 1960s as in the 1830s, there was no detailed advice on how to rear a limb-deficient child. Relying on common sense the mothers of upper-limb-missing babies started to stimulate the feet as a replacement for the hands, although this aroused anxiety in all of them. Nevertheless, four of

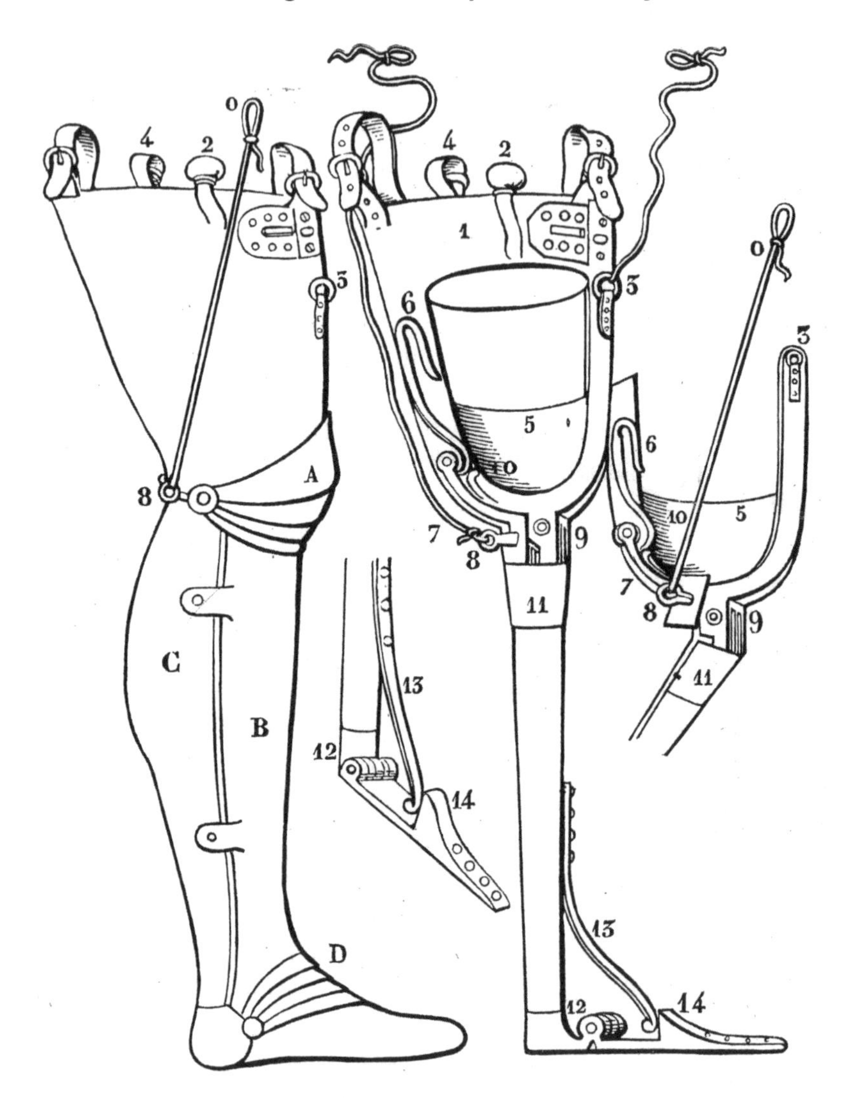

An artificial leg originally designed in the 17th century and still in use in the 1830s.

the eight upper-limb-affected babies spontaneously began to use their hands between five to eight months. All the parents at this point regarded future prostheses as the "new hope" and were impatient for their children to be fitted with them.

Children with upper-limb problems were given prostheses around the age of two years. When shown the artificial arms and

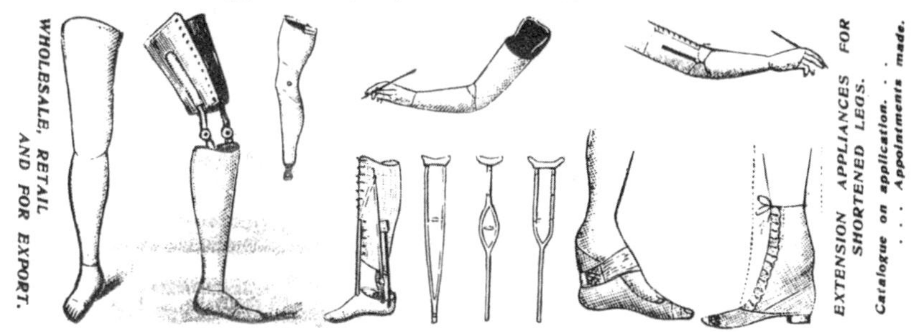

In the 19th century, sometimes rather bizarre to us, advertisements for artificial limbs appeared.

legs that their child would receive, six out of eight mothers were disappointed. They saw the prostheses as cold, hard, artificial and cumbersome. They complained the children were hard to caress – and that was especially true when children were fitted with hooks rather than artificial hands. The two mothers whose children were most like Arthur – i.e. they had upper and lower limbs missing – were the most anxious. This detailed research gives us some sense of what Arthur and his parents had to cope with 130 years earlier.

Boxwell really was a gifted therapist, though. He grasped depression and lack of hope was a huge risk for Arthur and he always wondered what might help. As soon as Arthur was three months old, Boxwell showed him the horses on the estates. When Arthur had learned to sit up, Boxwell held him on a small pony.

A few months later Boxwell took Arthur for his first ride. The doctor expected Arthur to be scared but, in fact, the boy loved being so high up. In the saddle Arthur was more or less the same height as a normal child would be. It was wonderful. Unexpectedly, Arthur turned out to have an excellent sense of balance. By the time he was two, he was able to sit on a pony. Boxwell set about designing a saddle, which would allow Arthur to ride alone.

The saddle was a basket, which could be tied fast on to the pony. Boxwell was nervous the first time he lifted Arthur into it and

MR. H. J. STUMP,

(Nine Years Pupil and Assistant to Mr. Fredk. Gray.)

NOT AN EXHIBITOR IN ANY EXHIBITION.

Constructor to Lord Hardinge.

ARTIFICIAL
LEGS, HANDS,
AND
NOSES.

Amputation below Knee.

With Knee-Joints and Thigh-Support.

LIMBS RE-ADJUSTED.

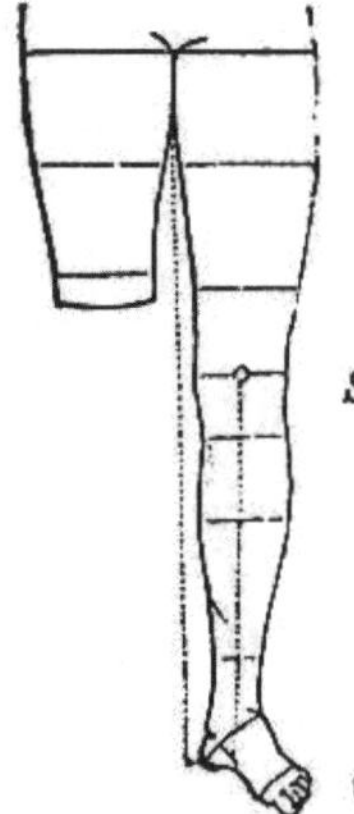

Spring and other Crutches.

Surgeons supplied with Diagrams for Self-measurement when the Patient cannot come to London.

SURGICAL INSTRUMENT MAKERS AND WHOLESALE HOUSES SUPPLIED.

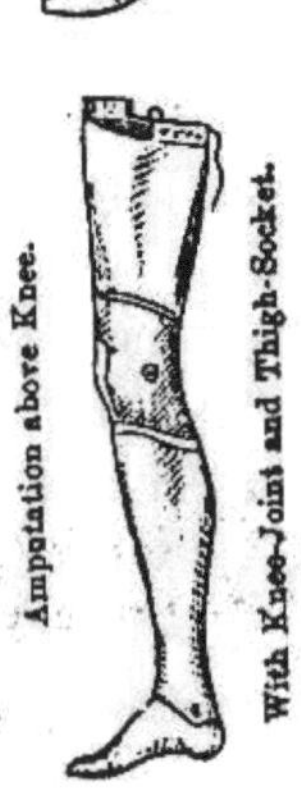

53, BOLSOVER STREET, GT. PORTLAND STREET, W.

(Facing Portland Road Station.)

ESTABLISHED FEBRUARY, 1863.

The author admits that he has been unable to verify that Mr Stump was really the name of this manufacturer. Few biographies answer every question. The ad is real enough, though.

tightened the straps which belted the boy in till he was sure the boy would be safe. The doctor then walked the pony slowly.

Arthur loved the feeling of being on the horse. He purred with pleasure. Over the next 12 months, Boxwell finessed the design and came up with a saddle, which was a box three sides of a square with a crupper. It had a breastplate to keep Arthur firmly in place. Boxwell described it as a single broad strap buckler across in front of Arthur which would prevent his falling out if the horse stumbled. The rein was a simple short one. Arthur could manage to hold the rein between the stump and the side of his body.

Next, Boxwell devised small hooks that were sown into the specially strengthened cuffs of Arthur's shirts. These hooks helped him hold the reins just using his right stump. As Arthur's stumps became slightly longer and much stronger, he could also use the hooks to pick up objects. Eventually, he learned how to fish with them.

All those devices would not have given Arthur confidence if he had been kept out of sight but Boxwell also insisted on the boy being taken into Ballyraggett and other nearby villages. Children were told they must not laugh or tease Arthur. He was the son of the local lord, after all. But it was hard not to admire the child perched in his saddle, managing somehow to control the pony.

Helping Arthur to ride was just one example of how imaginative Boxwell and Lady Harriett were. They were also quick to respond to "magic moments", to some surprising feat the child managed. They seized on what he had done, thought about it and tried to work out the next challenge. We expect normal children to develop skills at particular ages; with profoundly disabled children, parents often don't know what to expect. What was impressive about Lady Harriett and Boxwell was how much they noticed about how Arthur was developing.

Arthur's body might be disabled, but his mind was not. He was fascinated by the romance of his family's history. His father Thomas often stressed the centuries-old story of the Kavanaghs wasn't just an antiquarian hobby. He told Arthur he was in the middle of fighting with the Crown to re-possess the White Mountains which were close to the family estate. His sons would need to know their history intimately to defend their rights.

Crisis in Carlow

The position of the Irish landlords was under threat. Catholics were allowed to vote after 1827. Five years later, The Great Reform Bill enfranchised all those who owned £10 of property. The Catholic "Liberator" Daniel O'Connell had a large following and when he decided to stand for Carlow in 1832, he easily won the seat.

Thomas Kavanagh wanted to win Carlow back in the 1835 election but he entered the campaign in poor health. He was also unwilling to face up to political and social changes. He ignored the fact that he now needed to persuade more voters including many Catholics. His election address published in *The Carlow Sentinel* just asked people to look at his record. *The Carlow Sentinel* noted acidly: "With the security and self possession of his class he proposed no definite programme, merely mentioned his previous record which he did not elaborate on, as sufficient reason for voters to support him." *The Kilkenny Moderator* was kinder. Thomas was "the scion of the oldest family in the British Empire and possessed of a princely income." He had been generous enough to spend some of that princely income on improvements to the estate and on "promoting the comforts of his poorer neighbours." He deserved the votes.

The philanthropy cut no ice with the Catholic clergy, however. Father John Walshe who was the parish priest stood against Thomas Kavanagh in 1835. Walshe's nephew stood against Thomas Kavanagh's friend Henry Bruen for the second Carlow seat. Neither Thomas nor Bruen believed the Irish really deserved the new democratic rights granted by the Great Reform Bill. When the older Walshe came to talk to the Kavanagh tenants at Glynn, Thomas turned up with the militia. The soldiers marched the tenants back to Borris where they were "cooped" up and told they would not be un-cooped until they had voted the way Thomas and Bruen wanted.

Kidnapping voters was illegal even in 1835, but that was not the end of the matter. A few days after the cooping up, Walshe's nephew was found murdered at Kilgranny Bridge. Arthur's father and Henry Bruen were accused of being responsible for the killing. Daniel O'Connell demanded an inquiry. Thomas was suspended from Parliament while the accusations were investigated. He became gloomier and his wife was not that interested in consoling him, it seems.

Arthur passed from being a toddler to a little boy in a tense, unhappy atmosphere. Lady Harriett escaped partly by going sketching. Boxwell suggested she take Arthur with her on these expeditions round the estate. On one of those days, something decisive happened. Lady Harriett placed a brush in her son's mouth. He tried to draw with it and, then, dropped the brush on the blanket. Then, Arthur bent down and picked the paintbrush up between his stumps.

Lady Harriett was astonished. She put a sketching pad down for Arthur and was amazed to see he had enough control to dip the brush in the watercolours and start to doodle.

Later that day, Lady Harriett told Boxwell who admitted he had never imagined Arthur would be able to learn how to write. It was another moment his mother and Boxwell seized, the start of a great leap forward. If Arthur could pick up a brush, he could learn to write his letters. By the end of year, he could write all the letters of the alphabet.

Everyone had assumed that Arthur could never ride and never write. Maybe it was just as wrong to assume he could never walk.

The history of artificial limbs

Peg legs were known in the Middle Ages and they worked reasonably well for someone who had lost a leg either below or just above the knee. The usual amputee had three fully fit limbs. With one leg and two arms, you could generate enough motor power to swing one wooden leg forward and back.

With thousands of soldiers limbless after the Napoleonic wars, surgeons had every reason to focus on this area. Firms like Bigg and Sons in Leeds became expert makers of artificial limbs and Henry Heather Bigg was convinced the "mechanic" was as crucial as the surgeon in helping the injured. Bigg advertised his varieties of artificial legs and included testimonials from satisfied customers.

One aristocratic amputee needed a special stump to use while hunting. Any animal who thought his Lordship was easy meat because he only had one-and-a-half legs would soon get its come-uppance.

In later life, Arthur would have approved.

Bigg noted that patients who had "high" amputations faced the worst problems. He had studied disarticulation, the process of removing the bone. If the bone were removed, then the stumps rested more comfortably but the amputee had even less power. Even a few inches of bone provided some power, which made it easier to move artificial arms and legs.

There was also a market for artificial arms that allowed gentlemen to carry on. Gustav Ernst described an elaborate mechanism for a man who had lost both arms in a shooting accident. Cne of the advantages of the Ernst system was that you could still smoke. With one arm, you could still shoot.

Making a prosthesis for Arthur was much more difficult because he "was" really just a head to hip and groin. But he was to be treated by Ireland's best, Sir Philip Crampton and Dr Marsh, and Lady Harriett was sure her wonder boy would make it.

By the time he was 5 Arthur's arm stumps were 2 and 5/8th inches long and his leg stumps had grown to just over 4 inches. Dr Boxwell told Arthur's mother that Dr Marsh and Sir Philip Crampton were ready to make an "experimental application". Everyone was confident that Arthur who rides so well will have no problem walking.

The party travelled to Dublin by train, and took a hansom across the grey Liffey to Sir Philip Crampton's laboratory. It was filled with books, skeletons, pictures of skeletons, bones.

"So this is the little chap," Sir Philip bent down to Arthur's level. "You have to be prepared to be a patient patient. I assume you are clever enough to get the joke."

"Yes sir."

"Are you patient?"

"Yes sir."

"I need to take a cast," Sir Philip said.

"Thank you, doctor," Arthur's mother replied, more humble than she has ever been before.

Sir Philip applied wet clay round Arthur's leg stumps and told the boy to stay still. The clay itched. Arthur tried hard to control it but his stump was starting to twitch.

"Good boy," Sir Philip examined the cast and started on the left stump. When he declared Arthur has been a good boy, Lady Harriett puts a bonbon in his mouth.

A month later, the party makes the same trip and arrives back at the laboratory. Sir Philip beams as he points to the iron legs he had engineered. Each has a bucket of smooth metal; a criss cross of leather straps to lace Arthur's stumps in.

"I call them The Rockets after the new locomotive. They are the most ingenious legs," Sir Philip smiles. "You may touch them, Arthur. They will become part of your body,"

"I hope so, sir," Arthur says.

"You must try your hardest Arthur," Lady Harriett says.

"I will do my best, mama." It's true. He knows that she will love him so much if he passes this test.

Sir Philip eases the right stump into its bucket. The metal feels smooth but pinches against Arthur's skin. He itches again, he itches so much and he can never scratch like anyone else.

"Splendid," Sir Philip ties the criss cross of straps. Then he fits the left stump into its bucket. He pats the metal affectionately. "If this works young man, we shall both be famous and we shall be giving hope to many others. Try to get up."

Arthur makes an enormous effort to push himself out of the chair but the iron is too heavy.

"Arthur you are not trying," his mother says.

Despite the fact that Arthur had no arms, he was able to pull himself up out of the chair. But the child does not say it. He is learning to be silent, learning "to murmur not" as he puts it in his diary.

"Patience is a virtue, Lady Harriett," Sir Philip puts his big hands round his shoulders and yanks him straight up. The sudden movement makes the top of the buckets jolt against Arthur's groin. He yelps with pain.

"God wants you to be brave, Arthur. I am praying to Him to give you the strength," Lady Harriett says.

Arthur stands up, his back leaning against Sir Philip's big hands.

"How does it feel?"

"Very good, sir" Arthur lies. Later he will admit that he did not dare say he was terrified he would keel over. He dreaded trying to move. It wasn't like being on a pony. The legs would slip out under him any moment. Everyone was watching. Would the wonderful cripple boy move? He can't budge. If Sir Philip stops holding him he will topple over.

"Perhaps you should try a few steps, Arthur," his mother says.

"I think we should wait till the little chap feels comfortable. You don't have to do anything in a hurry."

If his mother were not there, Arthur would wait, just stand, get used to this weight. But she wants him to move. He has learned to ride, to draw, to write. Walking should be possible. He nods to Sir Philip. Gingerly, he lets go of the boy's shoulder.

"Just move your right leg forward," Sir Philip says, "in your own time."

In his own time? He is doing this in Crampton's time, in his mother's time, in Boxwell's time.

"Arthur, Sir Philip has worked so hard," Lady Harriett insists, "you must try . . . It's just like riding,"

"Please, Lady Harriett. We are not the ones wearing the legs," Sir Philip points out.

Arthur takes a deep breath. "I'll be fine," he lies. Now it's his turn to pray to God. Give me the strength to yank my little right stump forward and take the leg with me. He even prays to his stump, begging it to behave properly and shift forward. He concentrates his entire mind on the few inches of his stump and wills it, wills himself to lift the leg up.

For a second, a miracle. The leg rises, it moves up in the air.

Then, Arthur does not have the strength. A second before it happens, he knows it will happen and he can't stop it. But nothing prepares him for the ludicrous clank as he falls in a heap and knocks his head on the metal of the right leg.

"I hate them," Arthur cries.

"You're not a baby, Arthur," his mother snaps.

"I just can't move them,"

"You will have to practice, practice makes perfect."

"Yes, mama".

Sir Philip helps Arthur up from the floor. "We can't expect to get it right first time. Your mother's quite right, practice will help. Dr Boxwell will help. I dare say prayer will help too. You're trying to do something remarkable."

"I promise to try." The good cripple boy always does his best to please. As Sir Philip gets him up, Arthur thinks of mediaeval knights in their suits of armour who can't have found it easy to rattle their sabres in their metal. The honour of the Kavanaghs is at stake. He can't fail. His mother will be so unhappy if he does not walk.

"May I try again," the willing, good boy smiles. Everyone is pleased at his pluck.

Arthur manages to move the right leg. Then he freezes again. He tells himself it can't be so hard to drag the left leg one step forward. Before he starts to move the left leg, Sir Philip sees he is about to fall again. He catches him before he clatters to the floor.

"New things take time. Take them back to Borris and practise and come back in a month," he says. He pats Arthur on the back.

Boxwell gathers the legs, the buckets, some oil, which is apparently useful in cleaning them. Sir Philip gives Arthur a bonbon.

As they return on the train to Borris, Lady Harriett is silent. As they reach Ballyraggett, she reminds Arthur that his father is ill. The best tonic for him would be to see him walk across a room. Arthur practices for hours. His stumps chafe against the metal and Anne has to rub ointment into them all the time. Lady Harriett does that too.

Arthur's diary

After a month, I have made progress. I still can't push myself up to stand but if someone levers me up, I can stand on those legs. Holding on to Boxwell or Melrose or William, I can walk across a room like a lolling metal monster. On my own, I can never take more than three steps without falling over. No one ever laughs. No one complains.

"I can see you are trying," my mother says.

I want to tell her how much I hate looking in the mirror. I'm a freak. The top half of my body is normal since I'm used to having no arms. The bottom half looks like a metal monster.

My mother begs me to walk in front of my father. I want to please them but I'm scared. I explain to him I am still learning how to do it. He is sitting in his great red armchair, drinking rum. My mother says I've been practising very hard for him. I manage four steps before I fall to the ground.

"Well done, Arthur," my father says. He tells me to come closer and he puts his arms around me. He's trying not to cry because he knows I will never walk with these contraptions

"Arthur just needs to try more," my mother smiles.

Father and son – the illness of Thomas Kavanagh

Lady Harriett could not accept that her wonderful boy would not manage the artificial legs. She and Dr Boxwell often took him to Dublin. Boxwell tried to explain the mechanics of Arthur's problem but Lady Harriett was stubborn and she had faith, faith in God, faith in Arthur. Crampton explained it was very hard for Arthur to generate the muscle power needed to shift the legs. The great surgeon was always gentle with the boy because he saw how much Arthur did not want to disappoint his mother. Crampton even suggested abandoning the experiment to Boxwell but Lady Harriett would never admit failure.

The struggle with the legs only added to the gloom at Borris House. Thomas Kavanagh had survived the inquiry into the election practices of 1835 but he was too ill to go to London and take his seat at Westminster. He celebrated his 60th birthday in a bitter mood in April 1837. Five weeks later, he was dead.

Arthur was six years old. He was heart-broken by his father's death. It was to prove a turning point in his life. Lady Harriett had never felt Thomas was the love of her life. She missed her cosmopolitan life and now she no longer had to be marooned in Borris if she could make respectable arrangements for her children.

Tom and Charley were going to Eton. Within two months of Thomas's death, Lady Harriett decided her daughter Hoddy needed to go to boarding school. She was recommended one in Torquay. But she had to inspect the place first.

She worried she had been pushing her son too hard, so Lady Harriett decided to take Arthur with her and Hoddy. They took the ferry from Dublin and, then, the train to Torquay. Lady Harriett soon discovered the problems of travelling with Arthur. People stared, sometimes they mistook him for a baby and were amazed when he carried on a conversation, sometimes they wanted to discuss how the "tragedy" had happened. It was a little embarrassing and Lady Harriett did not like that. Arthur, on the other hand, loved being with his mother. Hoddy was enrolled in the school and so on the way back to Borris, Arthur had his mother all to himself and he promised to try again with the metal legs.

Once they returned to Borris, Arthur kept his promise. As he had grown, the whole exercise of taking a cast had to be repeated again. Crampton was less optimistic but he did not refuse the commission. Lady Harriett then employed a new surgeon, Reynolds, who claimed he could produce a better leg. For two years she pleaded, nagged and, then, punished her son. Finally she lost patience. She was angry with him. He was being lazy, he was being wilful. She refused to see that the legs didn't work because they couldn't work. For once, Arthur could not triumph over his disability.

When Lady Harriett realised he was never going to walk, her attitude to Arthur changed. She had tried so hard with him and it just had not worked. Hoping for a miracle had been the main reason she had stayed in Borris after her husband died. Now she knew the truth; God would deny her. Once she no longer believed Arthur would walk, she made appropriate arrangements for his education away from Borris. Then, she could return to her natural habitat, the salons and soirees of Europe.

As it happened a distant relative ran a small school at Kildare, 12 miles from Dublin. So at the age of nine Arthur was sent to be taught by Dr Greer. A number of Arthur's cousins were also studying there. Dr Greer was a rather stuffy clergyman but he liked Arthur and he was kind. He made all the children promise not to tease the boy. Greer said he would whip any child who made unpleasant remarks.

Lady Harriett was satisfied that Arthur was in good hands and so she was free to carry out God's will. If God had not wanted her to travel, He would have put more obstacles in her way.

Over the next 10 years Lady Harriett would be away from Borris far more often than she would be there. It is easy to paint her as an uncaring mother and, even, something of a hypocrite. Psychologists and social workers understand more now about the pressures parents of disabled children face. The most loving parents need to get away sometimes as their children demand so much. Lady Harriett felt cheated. Arthur had proved he could do so much and, then, he had given up on trying to walk.

Arthur was very upset when his mother told him she was leaving. She told him to write to her. It wasn't just being left, it was also not knowing when she would come back. When the Victorian upper classes travelled they did not have a schedule. They were away for months, even years.

Arthur was to suffer *separation anxiety* for years. The Victorians didn't have the jargon but the concept is simple. Children need mothering and fathering. If they are left, they feel wounded. The wounds are conscious and unconscious. Some psychiatrists like John Bowlby (1960) argue separation anxiety leads to delinquency. But even children who don't misbehave are scarred by being left. Research on children of divorced parents (Burgoyne 1972) shows they often blame themselves when one parent leaves home. The psycho-logic of the child is stark; I must have done something wrong to have driven him or her away. Usually, the child has no idea what he or she did that was wrong but Arthur knew perfectly well. He had been born without limbs and he had not mastered the metal legs his mother dreamed would save him. No wonder his father had died and his mother was now in Paris or Palermo.

Between 1839 and 1843, Arthur was taught the conventional curriculum at Dr Greer's academy. He learned Latin, Greek and history. He continued to study his family's glorious past. Arthur had a gift for languages and also for maths. He was so much better at sums than the other children that he even gave his cousin Sarah maths lessons.

Arthur wrote many letters to his mother and nearly all asked when his dear mamma might be coming back. Lady Harriett avoided giving definite answers. The roads were bad; she had to visit another spa, her presence was required at the salon, at the soiree, at the palace. She was no longer the woman who had taken her small son sketching, who had rubbed ointment into his stumps to ease the pain of the metal legs.

Living away from Borris made Arthur aware of how important it was to look smart. He became very careful about the way he dressed. He was always well groomed, said his sister Hoddy. "He wore a black kilt, gracefully covering his limbs like a robe."

Greer's academy was relatively informal and Arthur soon became its dominant personality. He was often the one who had ideas for adventures and games. But the self-confidence that gave him did not console him.

For much of the time Lady Harriett was away, the political situation in county Carlow was very volatile. Arthur would have also had to cope with those stresses. Soon after the "troubles" began again in Northern Ireland in 1969, psychologists noticed children were being affected. In 1973, Morris Fraser, a Belfast psychiatrist, wrote *Children in Conflict.* He argued that the constant threat of violence was hurting children. They had nightmares, suffered crippling anxiety and easily became violent. In the 1980s, after 15 years of violence, three psychologists from Queens University – Liz McWhirter, Karen Trew and Mary McIvor – re-examined his ideas.

Nevertheless, the psychologists wondered if Fraser might not have been too grim in his conclusions. For example, Trew asked children to complete a number of sentences that described what they were like. A 9-year-old boy, for example, said he saw himself as a human being, a person, a boy. He stated – I go to school, I like food, I like building, I hate work, I hate carrots, I like pies, I go to bed, I clean my teeth, I go to Mass, I brush my hair. For Trew, the moral was that life went on despite the conflict. The violence was all around and yet, somehow, children grew up.

Arthur, however, was not an ordinary boy like Trew's 9-year-old subject. Arthur was steeped in Kavanagh history. He could trace his descent from the old kings of Leinster. Being close to conflict left him very aware of his class and the threats it faced. He also knew that in any real violence, he would be physically helpless. In later life, he always saw the battle between his class – the great landowners – and the Catholics as simple. It was them or us. The landlords or the tenants. Catholics or the Protestants. You had to be careful not to give too much away to those who wanted to destroy you completely.

In 1840 Arthur lived through two crises on or near the Kavanagh estate. First, there were riots at the White Mountains close to Borris. The Kavanaghs had claimed the right to pasture horses and cattle on the slopes of the White Mountains for over two centuries. In 1833, Thomas paid the Crown £5000 for the property. Then, the Kavanaghs' land agent, Charles Doyne, fenced in some of the land and chased away anyone who tried to put animals to graze on the hills.

Second, the 1840 election would lead to more violence than there had ever been before on the White Mountains. Daniel O'Connell, Thomas Kavanagh's opponent in 1835, put up his son to fight the Carlow seat. Henry Bruen had been cleared of kidnapping voters in 1835 and stood again. Incorrigible, Bruen got the militia to coop up 200 Kavanagh tenants again so that they would learn to vote the right way.

On May 12th a large crowd assembled on the White Mountains and attacked Denis Ryan and Edward Lawler who were working for Doyne. Doyne asked the Lord Lieutenant for militia to restore calm but *The Carlow Sentinel* noted that "the Lord Lieutenant whose conduct has been anything but candid or honourable" did not interfere "to check these lawless men."

There were more riots on June 6th. Shacks and huts on the mountains were destroyed. *The Sentinel* again blamed the laziness of the Lord Lieutenant. *The Reign of Terror in Carlow*, as a book described it, attacked the authorities in Dublin for not taking the plight of Carlow seriously. In June, O'Connell arrived in the county as well as "notorious agitators who possessed neither character nor stake in the country and were reckless in the sanguinary course they pursued," it claimed. The agitators didn't mind shedding blood.

O'Connell denounced Henry Bruen who had stood with Thomas Kavanagh as "unfit to live in a country such as Ireland." If the electors did not vote the Catholics in, the godless Tories would "decimate their priests," he said. Strangely, O'Connell also proclaimed his loyalty to the Crown. The Tories would also "poison the Queen who had sent him to command the people everywhere to rise en masse against their hereditary oppressors." But "even with stimulants such as these the population could not at first be induced to proclaim war to the knife against the gentry," *The Reign of Terror* noted. But O'Connell pressed on.

"I call on their priests to stand up in the face of this meeting and answer for their flocks. I am at a loss to know how they can account with their God if they permit their flocks to vote for Colonel Bruen," thundered O'Connell.

On June 14th, O'Connell addressed a huge crowd in Bagnalstown and said "the blood of Father Walshe is still unavenged. He was brutally murdered by the Orangemen. Will the people of Carlow vote for the faction that murdered their priests in cold blood?" The crowd demanded revenge, which was just what O'Connell wanted.

A week later, O'Connell assembled 20,000 men and led them to Borris. Some were armed with pikes; others with "formidable bludgeons". There was looting, fighting and a number of deaths.

The end of June saw the dramatic trial of the White Mountain trespassers before a jury of six Catholics and six Protestants at Wexford Sessions. The *Carlow Sentinel* said "it was expected that a verdict would be found without a dissentient voice" and that no politics would sully "a simple case" of whether or not the accused caused a riot and assaulted the land agent's men. In the end, the Catholics all refused to convict and the rioters of the White Mountains went free.

In the midst of such turmoil, it's hardly surprising that Arthur wanted his mother. His letters – he was only 9 years old – show that he minded badly that he was seeing far less of her than her other children. He wrote:

I suppose you did not intend to bring us to Borris this summer therefore I will see neither Hoddy nor Charley. I am very sorry.

I suppose you intend going abroad with Tom and Charley. May we soon to Torquay? You cannot think how happy it would make me to live at dear Borris again, not writing to one another but having a pleasant chat at home.

Lady Harriett's response was to complain that Arthur's letters were too short. Arthur was beginning to understand that humour had its uses in dealing with his mother and he replied that as her letters were brief, this "was a bit like the story of the pot calling the kettle black."

Arthur had lost his father, his mother was away and seemed to be favouring his brothers and sisters. Even if he hadn't been disabled, it would have been a lot to cope with. At this time, in his diary, Arthur admits there was one incident where he did not behave with his usual restraint. This seems to have been the only episode in his childhood where he behaved violently. He passed it off as just a lark, part of a game. That only shows how smart he was. Again, based on his journal, I make an "imaginative leap".

Arthur's diary: March 1840

When I have a house of my own, it will have no mirrors.

My cousin, Jonah, would often look at me and laugh. I did not want him to see me turning the pages of the book I was reading. The hooks made it possible but I looked like the mechanical monster. He was huge, broad-shouldered, tall.

"I hate reading. Swots read. You're not just a cripple but a swot, you'll never be a man like me," Jonah laughs. He often compared how tall he was and how small I was.

"I don't just swot."

If I had arms I'd punch him. Sometimes I don't know what corner of my mind makes me speak. I say, "I bet I know more dirty words than you."

"I bet you don't."

"Why don't we see? Are you scared?"

"How could anyone be scared of you?"

Again I don't know which corner of my mind or mouth is at work. I say "What would you most like to do?"

"I'd like to throw you across the room like a ball," Jonah says and, pauses. "I know that's not very noble but you asked. I know you'd like to hit me but you can't." He's no fool.

I had seen Hoddy put on an earring and I suddenly knew. If I had a pin in my mouth and Jonah were strapped down, as they'd tried to strap me in those legs, I could pierce his ears. "I'd like to pierce your ears and make you wear earrings."

"That's very strange," Jonah says, "I suppose if you're a cripple, you're bound to be strange."

"Do we have a wager? The one who knows more dirty words will be allowed to do what he wants. We tell no one, of course."

"You never have sneaked. I'll give you that, Arthur", he laughs. "Are you sure? I win and I can throw you across the room."

"Like a ball. And if I win I pierce your ears."

"I'm shaking with fright. How could you possibly do it?"

"With my teeth. I've got perfect teeth." Jonah puts his hand on my mouth and inspects my teeth. "If you'd let go of my teeth, I think you should go first," I smile.

Jonah seems very pleased. "You don't know any dirty words, do you? Once I start, you can't change your mind. You'll be sorry," he puts on a polite menacing voice. The cripple's meant to quake.

"I won't change my mind"

Jonah pauses and, then, as if he's letting me into the holiest of holies, the secret of secrets, he starts his list. "There's damned and bloody and God's teeth."

"Those are hardly dirty words."

"You're not supposed to say them," Jonah insists. "So what do you know?"

He didn't know, of course. When I was a baby, my father insisted that I be trained for the toilet like any child. He had an especially low water closet built that I could clamber on. But there is one thing a man with no arms and legs cannot do for himself, despite the mechanical ingenuity of our age – wipe his own bottom. My father had read that Roman senators had body servants and he decided a man should attend to these duties. When I was two years old, Anne was told it would be indecent for her to do such things. The honour – and my father thought it was an honour – would go a loyal manservant in his 50s, Melrose.

Melrose was gaunt and devout. All the crevices of the body had been designed by God. Dr Boxwell impressed on Melrose the need for hygiene. I couldn't wash myself, of course, so Melrose did it, three times a week, behind the ears, beneath the balls.

"Had a good shit then, master Arthur", he usually asked when I'd done on the water closet.

I never knew what to say to that.

"I suppose you want me to wipe your arse," Melrose would add.

I never knew what to say to that either.

As he wiped and washed me, Melrose couldn't stop babbling. Perhaps it was the strangeness of it all. It was from him that I learned.

"That master Arthur is your prick, or your lance or your weapon. And I bet his not so very tall Highness hasn't a fucking clue what else do you use it for?"

"You pass water with it."

"Piss is the word. But pissing is not the only thing it's good for. Don't you use your eyes when you walk round the fields. Prick or lance or member is also used – and this isn't a word to use in the drawing room – to fuck girls. Cows fuck, horses fuck, humans fuck. We're just as animal as the giraffe or the hippopotamus. That's why we need to pray to save our souls," he added.

Melrose warned me never to use these forbidden words. Not to my father, not my brothers, not even to Dr Boxwell. My mother would faint if she heard them though he was not sure she would know what they meant.

"I said bloody," Jonah said, "and damned. What do you say? You don't know one word see."

"You're wrong. Fuck, piss, lance, shit, cunt, prick – and arsehole. I think it makes seven to your two."

"Never heard of them. You've made them up."

"I didn't."

"I'll go look in the Dictionary." Jonah ran to the library and returned with Dr Johnson's Dictionary. He started with A – and

there was no arsehole. He was beside himself with pleasure by the time he had reached P and there was no piss.

"Are you ready, Arthur," he said.

It hadn't occurred to me they wouldn't be in the dictionary. Dictionaries were not the kind of subject I discussed with Melrose.

"They're not in the dictionary because they are dirty. I assure you on my word as a gentleman that these are the very dirtiest of words."

"What do they mean?"

I explained the meaning of each.

"I don't believe you, Arthur. Where would you have found out from?"

I was not going to get Melrose into trouble. As Jonah said, I wasn't a sneak.

"If you won't tell me how you found out about them, I assume you're lying. But I'll be very fair. You are a cripple after all. I'm seeing father on Sunday and I'll ask him."

That Sunday, after Church, Jonah asked to talk man to man with his father. Lord Dufferin was so appalled by the stream of swear words his son uttered, he slapped Jonah and told his tutor to whip the sin out of his son. Jonah was not a sneak either and did not explain our wager.

The next time I saw him, there was a new respect in his voice.

"Where did you learn them Arthur?"

"Telling you that wasn't part of the wager."

"I didn't expect to lose, Arthur. You out-foxed me. Well done. Well, when do you want to torture me?"

We agreed on the following Tuesday. I paid the blacksmith two sovereigns for his silence. He provided me with a lance and a brazier as well as a set of straps.

Jonah arrives in my room wearing a plain white shirt. He is scared, I'm pleased to see that. He lies down on the table. I insist Grace and Sarah strap him in. I say it is to make sure he shouldn't be hurt more than necessary but I know I like seeing him tied down like one of the illustrations in a book I have seen about the cruelties of the conquistadors.

I pick up the pin between my teeth. Grace checks no one is coming. If anyone interrupts us, we will say we are rehearsing a scene from the torture of the heathen savages.

I hold the pin in my mouth while the girls pinion Jonah.

I imagine all my strength flowing into my gums. The skin of Jonah's ears is stretched tight by the girls.

"I'm just preparing the pin."

"Do it for God's sake," Jonah closes his eyes.

I breathe deeply. Jonah clenches his teeth. He will do everything not to scream. I butt my head forward. I get the aim true with the pin. Blood spurts from his ears.

I'm disappointed. Jonah doesn't scream.

I move round to his left ear. The girls hold him down again. Sarah places a second pin in my mouth. She whispers "I know you want him to scream."

This time I gather even more strength in my lips and butt his ears harder.

"That hurts," Jonah yells.

"Don't make bets you can't lose, Jonah," I say. I don't add what I really feel. It's great, better than fishing out a trout and watching it dangle on the line till it flaps dead.

Jonah touches his ears gingerly. He is bleeding but gets up. He feels the blood trickle on to his cheek. He starts to walk away.

"That isn't all we bet," I remind him. He turns back, miserable. The girls laugh. They dangle in front of his face the long red earrings they have chosen.

"You have to stay still, Jonah," Grace says. She dabs some alcohol to disinfect the bleeding ear.

Once, they have fixed the earrings on Jonah I tell him to look in the mirror.

"Next time you want to laugh at me, remember how you look now." Jonah can't stand it any more. He picks me up and shakes me. He wants to throw me across the room and break my skull.

"If you throw Arthur across the room, I'll never forgive you," Sarah says.

"You're a nasty little boy, Arthur" Jonah shouts. But he puts me down, recovers himself. "I shouldn't have done that. You won fair and square."

I feel a little ashamed of myself. But sometimes, the peg legs, half arms, blind as bats, deaf as posts, need to make normal people bleed.

The missing mother

Arthur's letters and diaries never offer an explanation for this strange and disturbing incident. He dismissed it as high jinks and said it showed how nimble he could be. The need to inflict pain suggests perhaps Arthur did not find it easy to adapt to his mother's absence. In one letter to Hoddy, he noted "I am often inconsistent and have to fight back a fierce pride. I terribly want things which are impossible to have."

In 1841, Lady Harriett did come back from Europe. Arthur was overjoyed even though she insisted he try again with the artificial legs. She attended some of the early fittings with the new surgeon, Reynolds, but she was not as determined to get Arthur to walk as she had been before. At the end of the year, she headed for the Mediterranean. She told Arthur he was not to give up on the legs but once she was away, he felt under much less pressure.

On April 13th 1842, Arthur wrote to his mother saying that he and Anne had been in Dublin for a week while Reynolds tried to fit new legs. Once more, he could not manage it. Arthur had spent four years trying to learn to walk with different kinds of artificial legs and he couldn't bear to keep on trying. For Arthur giving up on the legs was a relief.

Not being able to manage the legs did not stop Arthur learning to fish, using the hooks to help him hold the rod. He also loved going hunting with Greer and with Boxwell but everyone assumed he could never hold a rifle.

With Lady Harriett away again, the sad letters started again. By now though Arthur was smart enough to inject a little teasing. He wrote:

My Dearest Mamma,

I suppose this will be my last letter to you as I hope soon to have the happiness of seeing you once more at dear Borris. Anne and I have been obliged to stop in Dublin with Reynolds for a week as he could not make my new legs without me. Oh dear Mamma you can't think how much I long for your return which I hope will be soon, please God. I have written to Tommy and Charley begging they would not let you stop at Geneva but to come home quick.

Lady Harriett did not even bother to return for Arthur's confirmation, an event that the Victorians took extremely seriously. He minded. Over the next 4 years there are many letters to her in Paris, Geneva, Florence, Rome and other destinations. Some make simple demands. For example, Arthur asked "I wish you would buy me some pencils and 3 or 4 brushes of different sizes." The other children – Charley, Tom and Hoddy – were often allowed to accompany Lady Harriett but the only trip Arthur took in those years was a visit to Brighton with Anne Fleming.

Dizzying about the Mediterranean meant, of course, Lady Harriett didn't attend to her duties as the mistress of Borris. She did not turn up for the harvest festivals, so it was left to Arthur to inform her of "the admirable manner in which your son represented his absent family."

But sometimes Arthur couldn't produce the humour. Some of the phrases in his letters to his mother are very raw. "Will you write somewhat oftener," he said and added, "when may we expect you home or do you intend coming at all?"

Though Lady Harriett was disappointed in her son, she did one interesting thing. She gave Arthur some land, which he could call his own, and some livestock. She also demanded detailed accounts. When he was 12 he sold his wheat for £8.58 and bought some pigs. He sold the potatoes to Doyne for £16. The profits went to charity. But her gift hardly made up for the years of her absence.

Lady Harriett did finally come back in 1844. Doyne suggested she hold a party for the workmen and tenants. In November a feast was served for 250 people. The barns were decorated and chandeliers hung. A "sprightly band" played. Tom and Charley were away at school and so, when the tenants proposed the health of the Kavanaghs, it was left to Arthur to respond. The 13-year-old had done it before but now, in front of his mother, he managed it very well. He drank to the health of the tenants.

These celebrations were moving for Arthur. He was always to believe there was a deep bond between all those who worked the land. The landlord had a duty to look after the tenants and the tenants had to love, honour and obey their betters.

Lady Harriett was impressed by Arthur's speech but it also made her oddly suspicious. Arthur was unnaturally good with words. It made her feel he was not really sincere.

Disabled people often speak of the need to hide their feelings. Not showing how different or how sad you feel is a survival strategy. In the letters he wrote to his mother, Arthur increasingly masked his pain. On the first page of a diary he started when he was fifteen, he wrote something about secrecy.

Though dark my path and sad my lot
Let me still and murmur not.

He murmured to no one. 20th century psychologists invented a cluster of concepts – repression, denial, sublimation – which have a simple basis. We displace or convert emotional pain and energy into something different. In the 19th century, human beings, and their souls, were supposed to be less hidden. As before, I think it's useful to look at Erikson's notion that we consciously and unconsciously choose radically different psychological directions. Arthur could give in to misery and he could make people feel sorry for him, or he could both cope, sometimes pretend to cope and not display his misery. By the time he was 10 Arthur had learned to compensate for many of his disabilities. He could show the world an acceptable face, the wonderful cripple boy who was clever, charming and triumphed over his enormous handicaps. It was a performance that needed steely self-control – and it was a performance he couldn't always give. Especially to himself. Sometimes he got so tired, he became very depressed but even then he used a word to describe these moods that didn't sound so bleak. He often said he felt "seedy". Nevertheless, he usually managed to keep – and to appear – in control.

In his late teens, Arthur came to adore two physical activities – sailing and hunting. Both allowed him to feel much more the master of his fate. His idea of a blissful day was a day spent potting pigs, snape, wigeon and anything else that moved naturally as he could never move. It is reasonable to argue that he was probably the greatest marksman ever who had no arms and no legs. He had mastered skills no one imagined he ever would. Hunting also let out his dark side, his violence. But as we shall see in the next chapter, Arthur found there was another kind of physical activity which eased his pain and that was one he had to keep very secret in the buttoned-up Ireland of 1845. By the time he was 15, Arthur understood that he loved and needed sex.

Chapter 4

Sons and mothers

In March 1845, Arthur celebrated his 14th birthday. His mother had returned to Borris and she decided it was time for Arthur to leave Greer's informal academy. Most Victorian men of Arthur's class went to Eton, Harrow or other boarding schools. Many of these were cruel places. One pupil at Eton complained to his father that he was beaten day in day out by the masters and prefects so much so that he became an emotional wreck. British upper class men tended to have their first romantic and sexual experiences with other boys and that left many wary of women. Greer's academy was a kind of boarding school but the Reverend had both boys and girls as his pupils. Unlike many Victorians of his class, Arthur was never afraid of women and, from his mid teens, he had an eye for women and a strong sexual drive. Girls made him less depressed. Local gossip suggested that his very helplessness made him attractive. It was unusual, almost exotic. The daughters of the local farmers were not the only ones taken with him. Lady di Bresci spoke of the real beauty of Arthur's face and of his splendid voice. And like many teenagers sex was to get Arthur into trouble with the adults.

Children who suffer separation anxiety and feel they have been left become ambivalent about their parents. They are angry with them and they want to please them. In the next seven years, Arthur lived through some remarkable experiences but his brittle relationship with his mother would always trouble him.

The trip

Arthur had been riding out over Mullins. When he came back through the village, he saw wagons drawn up outside Borris. All summer the house had received deliveries – linens, medicines, map, creams, tents – which made it clear to Arthur that his mother was going away again and in more style than usual.

Lady Harriett summoned her family.

"I have often talked to you children about being at the ball before the Battle of Waterloo," Lady Harriett announced, as Melrose served oxtail soup.

William sat next to Arthur, his shadow who spooned the food in, dabbed the napkin against Arthur's lips, made sure the boy did not make a mess of himself. Arthur disliked his mother watching him while he ate as much as Lady Harriett hated it if food spilt on his clothes.

"I hoped Wellington would win but, of course, we were all a little in love with Napoleon," she paused. "I have decided not to tantalise you any longer. I am going in the footsteps of Napoleon. To Egypt. To the Pyramids. And we shall go to Jerusalem to see the holy places. It will be an uplifting trip. We shall visit the places our Lord lived in."

Everyone cheered. But Arthur was worried that he would be left behind, as usual.

After dinner, Lady Harriett told her other children to leave. She told the servant William to leave.

"Every time I am away, Arthur, I am glad to get your letters, even if they're short." Lady Harriett said.

"I always miss you, mamma, when you are gone."

"I have been studying, Arthur, if it might be possible for us to take you with us," she added.

Arthur was overjoyed but careful. He knew his mother did not like any kind of excess.

"I have not yet decided it is wise or practical. There may be medical objections."

"But I'm perfectly healthy."

"You aren't the best judge of that," she said sternly,"and you have no idea of what can happen in the tropics. Dr Boxwell told me about Mr Dadd." Richard Dadd was a promising artist who went to the Middle East to sketch the people and the pyramids. He became extremely agitated. When he returned to Britain, he went for a walk with his father in the peaceful countryside and slit the old man's throat. Dadd fled to France but was captured after a fight on a train. He spent the rest of his life in hospital, first at the Bethlem and then after Broadmoor was founded as one of its first patients. The case attracted great publicity in the 1840s. It suggested that "a touch of the sun" could send people over the edge.

Arthur argued that he did not get "agitated" and that he could not cut anyone's throat since he had no hands.

Lady Harriett was not impressed. She added that she believed Arthur was quite capable of inflicting harm – perhaps she had heard of the incident with Jonah.

Arthur added that he promised to be good and pleaded; "But I'd love to travel with you, Mamma."

"What you love and what's good for you are not the same. I worry about anything which could make your condition worse."

She then explained that Boxwell had told her that the doctors believed the sun had made Mr Dadd's brain boil. "To stop my own brain boiling," she said, "I have decided not to sketch in the sun and you can imagine how disappointed I am."

"I won't sketch, I'll wear wet cloths on my head all the time, Please mamma."

"Don't beg, Arthur. If you have to stay here in Borris, I expect you to accept your fate with grace."

"I won't argue, Mamma, and I'll pray. I'll pray that you take me and I'll pray that if you don't, I'll accept your decision with good grace."

"You always know the words to please people." Her smile suddenly clamped shut. "But I see into your soul."

For Arthur the problem was how to convince his mother that it would be safe to travel with him. If Arthur had had a hand, he would have reached out to touch her.

"I will tell William to come and fetch you." She walked out of the dining room.

Arthur clambered down from his chair and waddled on his stumps to the writing table. He took his pen between his stumps and started a letter to Boxwell. He begged the doctor to use his influence. Why give him an education if he was always to be stuck in Ireland where he could not see the wonders of the world?

Usually, Boxwell replied quickly. But not this time. Arthur suspected he and his mother were conferring, weighing the pros and cons of letting him travel, deciding his fate. Did he deserve to go with them? In the weeks that followed, more tradesmen from Dublin delivered tropical clothes for Tom, Charley and Hoddy. The children wore silks and veils, they danced down the staircases and through the corridors pretending to be Arabs. No one told Arthur anything. If he said anything to his mother, he worried she would get impatient and angry.

A week later, William ushered Arthur into the formal drawing room. His mother sat on the large yellow sofa, Dr Boxwell stood behind her.

"Dr Boxwell and I have not come to any decision yet, Arthur."

"Your mother has been to the East and she knows the problems," Boxwell smiled. "Let me give you an example. The flies. People swat the flies away. You can't do that so William will have to swat your flies away as well as perform all his other duties. The heat and dust makes people itchy. You can't scratch yourself. No one knows how the heat might affect you or infect you."

"So I'm never to leave Ireland," Arthur snapped and regretted it at once. "I am sorry, Mamma, it's just . . ."

"So this is you showing good grace."

"We sometimes can't help saying what's on our minds," the mollifying Boxwell pointed out.

"Arthur is usually excellent at hiding what is on his mind," Lady Harriett sniped.

"There's something else, something we don't talk about because we're so used to you," Dr Boxwell looked nervous.

"You wonder how they will respond to someone like me. I might be bad luck."

"Or good luck, Arthur," Lady Harriett put in, unexpectedly. "The Mussulmans apparently believe some cripples have been touched by God and are holy. I don't want to deny you the chance to see the East but . . ."

"You can send me back at any time, I won't make a nuisance of myself"

"Don't beg, Arthur. When you were small you never begged," she shook her head to remind him that, once upon a time, he was better, her marvellous cripple boy. "I will discuss it with the doctor." She took Boxwell's arm and they strolled out through the French windows into the garden. Arthur was left under the great blue domed ceiling, waiting again.

Arthur's diary

I call William and get him to strap me into my saddle. I have to be doing something other than wondering what they are saying about me. I gallop miles to the south, jumping hedges. Usually I ride carefully because it isn't easy for me to balance as the horse jumps. But I'm upset, I lose control of Bunny as she vaults over a low hedge. We fall. I smash my face against a stone and it starts to bleed. Bunny whinnies in pain. Blood flows into my eyes. Horse blood, human blood. I have no hands to brush the blood away. I can't undo the strap of my saddle. I'm attached to a horse. Bunny tries to get up on her broken fender and she falls.

I mustn't panic. Bunny thrashes in pain. I know I must calm her.

I nuzzle Bunny with my head, I coo to her.

I try to get up on my stumps, but the saddle is so heavy I fall over. It's like the iron legs. I can't stand and I can't stand it.

The pun makes me feel better. I pray God for help. There's no miracle. Bunny thrashes all the time and each thrash jerks me in the saddle. Every bone feels shaken.

Then, I see a girl walking in the distance. I yell, "Help."

She stops to see where the voice was coming from.

"Help," I shout as loud as I can. I am so low on the ground she can't see me.

"Where are you," she calls.

"I can't get up. Over here."

She starts to walk towards me. I keep on repeating "Over here." As she comes closer, I realise the girl is Mary O'Callaghan. She runs the last hundred yards and peers down at me.

"Mr Arthur, you look a fright."

"Can you please get me out of my saddle, Mary?"

"You look like a huge beetle," she grins. She's sixteen years old, a red head, down on her upper lip. "I'll have to carry you home. You're a heavy monster," she says. She unstraps me and cradles me in her arms, "and a dirty one."

Mary has to stop every quarter of a mile and put me down while she gets her strength back. We struggle back to her parents' cottage. She sends her mother to Borris to get help. She pours some water in a basin and washes the mud and sludge off my hands and face.

Mary watches her mother trudge away. "You need more than your face washed," she pours cold water from another two jugs into their largest basin.

"How do you wash, Mr Arthur?" I like her directness.

"My man undresses me and soaps me and washes me."

"Would you like me to do that," she asks.

"If you don't mind, I feel so dirty."

She undresses me and sits me in the basin. "I'm sorry the water's cold. I bet you have lovely hot water at Borris," she starts to splash me. Then she smiles, "I like having you at my mercy, Arthur."

"So I see," I said. I am embarrassed by the fact that as she washes my back and face, I develop an erection.

But she grins. "I think we better hide that," Mary drapes a tea towel round my "lance". It is a delicate moment. My lance is, like the rest of me, wet. We don't know what to say. "I better dry you," Mary adds.

"Does that tickle," she asks.

"Tickle isn't the word," I laugh. I am the son of the lord of the manor. "How long before your mother gets back?"

"I'm surprised at you, Arthur"

"You're the one touching me," I smile.

"I was drying you, Arthur." Suddenly Mary laughs. Then, she wraps me up in the family's big towel and carries me to the room upstairs. She lays me on the bed and let her dress fall to the floor. "We better be quick and you'd better control that thing of yours." Her hand grasps me and, then, she takes me inside.

By the time her mother returns, we are downstairs again, dressed, drinking tea, having a decorous conversation about crops – and the possibilities of the potato. But the moment I see Dr Boxwell come into the cottage with William and Mary's mother, I forget everything else.

"Did my mother decide, Doctor?"

"I reminded your mother of when you were just born, when we decided that you should have as normal a life as possible. With the right preparations and if you promise to obey her, she's agreed to take you."

I wish I had an arm to thump the table with joy. "You brought me luck Mary O'Callaghan."

"Where are you going," she said, "to Dublin?"

"No to the Pyramids of Egypt. Since you brought me luck, Mary, will you allow me to give you a present? You need to fish the coin out of my pocket."

She sticks her hand in my pocket and, as she feels for the coin, she strokes the top of my groin. I am purring with pleasure inside but I show nothing. Mary shows nothing. She's a poor farmer's daughter trying to extract a sovereign from the pocket of a rich boy.

"You're looking for a gold sovereign," I say calmly. Boxwell looks puzzled. He must not suspect a thing so I explain what might seem an extravagant gift, which he would report to my mother. "If it hadn't been for Mary I might still be lying in a ditch. She rescued me. She's been an angel of mercy."

Very primly, Mary kisses me on the cheek.

"I bet you've never been kissed by a girl before," she says impishly.

"I don't think I have," I reply, the pious cripple boy.

Dr Boxwell lifts me on to his horse. I insist we find Bunny first, which takes some doing in the dark. The poor mare has crawled a few feet from where we had fallen. She's in great distress.

"We need to put her out of her misery," I say.

"Would you like to help me shoot her," Boxwell says.

"Yes, it was all my fault."

"I think we can do it like this." He places his rifle between my body and my right stump. He has his finger round the trigger. I look straight at Bunny and pat the poor beast.

"The rifle will recoil. It'll be quite a force," Boxwell tells me.

Together we point the gun at Bunny's heart. He asks me if I am ready and, when I nod, he pulls the trigger. I am shocked by the power of the recoil and fall into the mud again. Boxwell laughs.

"It's not funny. We just executed a horse, a horse I killed because I was careless."

"You're funny, Arthur, falling down. Any human being falling on his bum is funny. I think you better not try to shoot ever again."

I nod, the cripple accepting his impossibles. I don't tell Boxwell that the only thing I have enjoyed anything as much as taking that shot was fucking. I was glad my mother is not there to see me in case she really can see into my soul and see that I have just become a man.

To the east

Arthur was only 15 when the family headed off to Egypt, taking the ferry to Haverfordwest. The preparations were complex. Lady Harriett insisted her children had to learn and so she took the Rev. David Wood as a guide and tutor. Wood was young, pious and ambitious; he and Arthur often quarrelled though they were careful not to do so in front of Lady Harriett.

The party stayed at the Hotel Wagram in Paris and, then, took the train to Marseilles. From there, they sailed on October 14th and, after a brief stop in Sicily, they landed at Alexandria 10 days later.

Alexandria had a small British community and the Kavanaghs were welcomed as grandees. Arthur was hailed as something of a prodigy. They travelled to Cairo where they visited the Pyramids and were duly awed by them. But their plans seemed foolhardy to the locals. Lady Harriett was told that no women had ever travelled down the Nile. There were no hotels. The river was dangerous. The party would have to sleep in tents. Lady Harriett countered they had come supplied with all the necessary equipment and she had no intention of leaving her youngest son behind.

When they sailed down the great river at the end of November, it was less than 25 years since Belzoni had found the first tombs in the Valley of the Kings and less than 50 years since Napoleon had marched into Egypt. When they stayed ashore, the Kavanaghs

A picture by the famous 19th century artist David Roberts of travels in the Middle East. The Kavanaghs would have experienced something very similar.

had a tent for the women, one for the men and one for the servants and the luggage. Lady Harriett seemed to enjoy the life of the camp.

Arthur enjoyed the Nile. He loved to watch the wildlife from the boat though his reasons we would not now find politically correct. "The best shooting in the world is to be found in the Nile – birds of all plumage in abundance, from the large white pelican to the beautiful green and gold humming birds." He was so entranced he was again reckless. When they moored at Luxor, he leaned too far out on the boat and tumbled into the river. With no arms he could not swim. He told Sarah Steele years later that he was sure he was going to drown but one of the Arab sailors jumped in the river and saved his life. The fact that he had nearly drowned did not make Arthur take fewer risks.

The party returned to Cairo but Lady Harriett was determined to visit Jerusalem. However, crossing the Sinai Desert to reach the Holy City was not simple. Artists like Dadd and David Roberts have left rather romantic impressions of the desert – exotic travellers, bleached rocks, camels at an oasis. The reality was harsher. The Sinai was unforgiving. Bedouins and bandits preyed on travellers. For once, Lady Harriett listened to advice and agreed they should travel with a number of others for safety so the Kavanaghs made their way across Sinai in a caravan of 60 camels. It was a wise decision; no one tangled with them.

Arthur was the only one of his party to learn any Arabic and he liked the Bedouin. "They are so good natured and hospitable," he wrote, "though they are ferocious and will attack travellers. They are, however, most chivalrous towards women and I attribute our safety in Bedouin territory solely to the presence of women in our party."

The party finally reached Jerusalem just before Easter 1847. The city was under the control of the Ottoman Empire. Psychiatrists today speak of the Jerusalem syndrome. The intense religious atmosphere affects some individuals who develop psychotic symptoms; every year, hundreds announce that they are or have seen Christ, Elijah, Moses, the angel Gabriel. It gets too hot, too theological and too violent. The Jerusalem syndrome was fluffing up the clergy in 1847, as Arthur and his family discovered on Good Friday.

In the evening, the Kavanaghs found about 3000 men, women and children asleep in one of Christendom's holiest sites, the Church of the Holy Sepulchre. They stepped over the sleepers to admire the Church. What happened then astonished Arthur. He wrote:

> *A Greek service had just ended and a troop of Turkish soldiers were doing their best to persuade the Greek monks to make room for the Latins who, though the chapel belongs to the Greeks, have always had a right to one Mass there on Good Friday. As a conflict was expected between the Greek monks and the Latin priests, the chapel was lined with troops. The cause of the discord is the removal of the Greek altar cloth by the Latins when they begin their Mass.*

Lives had been lost over the altar cloth, Arthur pointed out. When the Latin clergy arrived, the Greek priests rushed at them. The Turkish troops intervened. At that moment, the Pasha himself marched to the altar. Coolly, the Pasha "addressed both parties on the propriety of peace at such a time." The Pasha told the Greeks to allow the Latins to have their mass. He also said, "he would march off to prison any person who broke the peace".

To stop any more brawls about the altar cloth, the Pasha himself removed it "with the greatest coolness and dignity. The two parties looked very foolish at this finale," Arthur noted. The Christians were supposed to be civilised while the "heathens" were the brutes. The fiasco at the Church of the Holy Sepulchre showed the opposite was true. "We could not help feeling the disgrace to Christians that at such a time and in a place they considered so sacred, the peace could only be maintained by Mahommedan good sense," Arthur wrote. Lady Harriett and the Rev Wood wanted to tour every church but Tom, Hoddy and Arthur found visiting so many churches boring.

The Kavanaghs bought six horses in Jerusalem. Arthur waxed lyrical about one of them, writing that "his limbs are fine without a puff – his eye and the expression of his countenance fiery yet sweet." This was an odd phrase to use about a horse, Arthur admitted, but that he could not think of a better way of describing the animal.

Arthur was in high spirits. He rode the horse to Hebron where he bought a Bedouin costume. He immediately dressed himself up as an Arab. The party also bought a brace of horse pistols covered in silver as well as sabres, daggers and innumerable knives. On May 26th 1847, Kavanagh wrote to Charley, "I am sure you would enjoy the East immensely – the most delicious fruit and everything enjoyable."

It wasn't just the fruit that was delicious. The trip also confirmed something else about Arthur. He wrote to Charley from Jerusalem praising the beauty of the local girls. Lady Harriett would have been horrified if she knew her son thought of sex a good deal.

While they were travelling, disturbing news reached them and a conscientious landlord would have returned to Ireland. The famine was killing thousands. A distant cousin of the family was a curate in Westport and he was giving the last rites to 40 parishioners a day. The workhouses were overcrowded. But Lady Harriett decided to travel on to Constantinople where she visited the wife of the Pasha. Then, she took her family on to Trebizond on the Black Sea. They made their way back to Beirut, which they reached on September 24th. Letters told Lady Harriett her mother was dying but even that was not enough to make her return to Britain. They sailed back to Cairo where Arthur bought a new horse and, then, took a boat again down the Nile.

This second trip allowed Arthur to fulfil one of his ambitions. He had always wanted to learn to shoot and he persuaded his mother to let Lord Morton (who had joined their party) teach him. Arthur remembered his experience with Boxwell and worked out how he could use his right stump and the hooks on his cuff to pull the trigger.

His son, Walter, many years later wrote the best description of how Arthur handled a gun. "He used an ordinary gun rifle except the trigger guard could be turned back leaving the trigger unprotected. Balancing the barrel of the gun on his upraised left arm, the stock was pressed closely to the right shoulder by the right arm which was in a position to press the trigger when he wished to." Walter did not mention the hooks that Arthur sometimes used to press the trigger. "It was really wonderful how the balance of the gun was maintained when the explosion of shot took place."

For the rest of his life, Arthur would find killing animals blissfully relaxing.

The trip had improved Arthur's relationship with his mother, but ironically, that meant that she had more expectations of her son.

The Kavanaghs got back to Ireland late in 1847. As soon as he was back, Arthur became aware of the problems that the Famine had caused on the estate. He was surprised that neither his mother nor his grandfather, The Earl of Clancarty, seemed to feel they had to help their tenants. Despite the famine, Clancarty encouraged the land agent, Mr Doyne, to be tough with the tenants. Lady Harriett's main concern was that Doyne should keep collecting the rents.

Arthur disapproved of his mother's attitude. We have seen that he had been impressed by the experience of proposing the health of the tenants when he was 13 years old. But Arthur had no official role on the estate. Nevertheless, he got involved; he joined the Agricultural Society, which tried to perfect techniques for saving at least part of each diseased potato. Doyne was amused by Arthur's enthusiasm. Arthur insisted on riding round the countryside and he talked to tenants and especially to their daughters.

In 1848 Lady Harriett decided to return to Europe even though her father protested she was spending too much money. This time she left all her children at home as Ireland started to explode again.

In the early part of 1848, the authorities in Dublin decided to crack down on dissent. They prosecuted three nationalists for sedition including an M.P called William Smith.

The Smith O'Brien rebellion

In July Arthur went to stay with his great aunt, the Dowager Marchioness of Ormonde at Garryricken near Slieve Na Man Mountains. Historians emphasise that the Smith Rebellion was not much of a threat to the state. Most of those who might have rebelled decided to wait "till rifles are forged in Heaven and angels draw the trigger," wrote Robert Kee in his *History of Ireland.* Smith never had more than a hundred properly armed men to march up and down and, on the best days, he could also muster two hundred others who were armed with rusty mediaeval pikes. The most famous episode in the Smith rebellion, the "battle" of Widow Cormic's cabbage patch, isn't exactly heroic. It took place when the government sent police out to arrest a number of Smith's men. The police were outnumbered and took refuge in Widow Cormic's cottage. The widow was not at home but her children were inside. The police barricaded themselves in the cottage and used the children as hostages. The famous ditty went:

They hid behind the windows of the Widow
They fired across the shoulders of her kids

"The parish priests were to a man averse to rebellion," noted Reverend Fitzgerald who was in charge of the parish at Ballingarry, "for notwithstanding their antagonism to a harsh government, they took a more hopeful view of future relations with the English than later events justified." Fitzgerald did not think all landlords were bad. He had "a high regard for the more enlightened landlords" and he included the Kavanaghs among them.

Nevertheless, the rebellion is now seen by historians as an important event. The new Secretary in Dublin, Henry Lurcom, asked for scouts to patrol the Carlow area to look for the rebels' camps. Arthur had been frightened and fascinated during the reign of terror in 1840. Now that he was seventeen, he wanted to show he was as much a man as any other landowners' son so Arthur started to ride out at night to search for the rebels. He liked being a one-man spying operation.

When he was older, Arthur liked to boast of his role as a spy. He told Sarah Steele that one night he succeeded in getting "near the rebel outposts but he was discovered and pursued by some of their cavalry." The mood was ugly. If they caught up with Arthur, he might have been killed. But he was a good rider and his horse, named Bunny again, out-ran and out-jumped Smith's cavalry. Arthur led his pursuers through countryside where you had to jump over hedges and fences. Bunny was a brilliant jumper. Arthur had guessed right; Smith's rebels were riding clapped out nags that balked at jumps and so the self-appointed teenage agent got clean away.

But was spying for Queen and country Arthur's only motivation? The Reverend Fitzgerald who defended him because he "had been a good friend of Irish Catholics," was wry about Arthur's role as a spy. "His part in the affair has been somewhat magnified," Fitzgerald wrote. Arthur's mission was not always military. Arthur often rode out to "meetings with a certain young woman who had taken a fancy to the hapless crippled youth," Fitzgerald said. "I do not suppose that his family had any idea that the moon had conjured up for him other and more romantic attractions than that of finding a few of O'Brien's followers."

But by the end of the rebellion, Arthur had become less interested in politics. He had fallen in love. The girl who he met is one of the great mysteries of Arthur's life. Her name was Fanny Irvine. She was a friend of Hoddy's and the daughter of a local landowner. She was very different from the farm girls Arthur had been in the habit seducing. Fanny was a girl of his class. Arthur knew that he had to keep his meetings with her secret because any tryst would be serious and his mother would disapprove.

Fanny found Arthur mesmerising and she was not put off by his disabilities. They started an intense courtship. His first reference to Fanny comes in a letter written in 1850 to Hoddy. He asks her if Fanny was at a party in Dublin. "Please let me know what happened. I am sorry to hear of Fanny's bad spirits and I hope that now, the temptation being over she will rally again. Tell her so with my love." But what the temptation was, he does not specify.

This enigmatic entry has to be read together with another letter Arthur wrote to his sister Hoddy. It said:

> *Give my love to Fan and tell her, my dearest wife, that I have got her precious verbena safe and hope to bring it home and exchange it for a more substantial and lasting proof of her unalterable affection.*

The implication of the phrase "my dearest wife" is remarkable. It suggests that Arthur and Fanny were married or, at the very least, betrothed. I have found no evidence to suggest that actually happened so It seems most likely the young people had some kind of "arrangement" between themselves. In early 1848, Arthur believed his mother knew nothing about his flirtation with Fanny. But Lady Harriett made it her business to be well informed. She was employing the Reverend Wood and it is likely that she also paid William for information on her son. It came to an unpleasant climax in March.

Arthur's diary: March 31 1848

My mother calls me into the drawing room the day of my birthday. William carries me right up to her. On my birthday, she usually kisses me on the cheek.

Instead, she takes a step back. William places me in the red chair. He piles cushions under me so that I can sit up.

"I did not say you could place Mr Arthur in his father's chair, William," my mother says. "Mr Arthur can stand, William. Mr Arthur can perform many feats which would surprise the medical authorities."

I hate the ice in her veins voice. But I obey. I stand, dwarf-like, before her.

"You may go, William." Doors clang shut down corridors, up staircases, reflected in mirrors, echoing through the house.

"Look at yourself, Arthur," my mother barbs.

"I am not tall enough to see myself in the mirror."

"That is not as clever as you think," she sighs. "I expected high standards of you, Arthur."

"What have I done?"

"You know what you have done."

"All I know is I am accused. It's usual to tell the accused what they are accused of."

"Don't be impertinent Arthur."

"May I sit down, Mamma?"

"No."

Imagine what it feels to look at a room like a small child. The adults loom huge, menacing. You have to stare up at them.

"You know Miss Fanny Irvine."

Lady Harriett Kavanagh
Arthur's mother who danced at the ball on the eve of the Battle of Waterloo in 1815 and lived until 1885

I am relieved. I have only kissed Fanny or, to be precise, Fanny has kissed me since I am in no position to wrap my arms round an unwilling girl. If Mamma had any idea of my activities with Louise, Mary or Tinkerbelle, I would have been in for the high jump, which, of course, is beyond me.

"I feel so disappointed, Arthur."

"Mamma," I protest.

And, then, I stop. My mother stares at me. I see myself as she sees me. I am just 24 inches tall. How can a creature 24 inches tall, smaller than a big dog, expect to be petted, kissed, fucked? "Please don't be so cold, Mamma", I think – but I can't say the words.

My mother says nothing. She plays the silence of disapproval to perfection.

"I don't want to talk about it any more. I have arranged for you to leave Ireland," she says, not looking at me.

I realise it is easier now for her to be Mamma with ice in her veins than to show her real feelings. She used to love me. I remember how good that felt. Now, I don't just disappoint her, I disgust my mother. All I have done to deserve her disgust is to flirt with Fanny Irvine. Normal for a normal young man but obscene for me.

Mamma has loved me when I behave like a cripple should – meek, grateful, humble, and devout. Flirting is forbidden for a creature like me.

"I don't want to leave Borris," I say. I should beg for forgiveness, of course, but I will not. I may be only 24 inches, but I won't be the pleading for mercy cripple.

"It's not a question of what you want," she says. "You will travel with Tom and, of course, you will need a responsible tutor. The Reverend Wood has kindly agreed to travel with you."

"You know I don't like Wood."

"It is not a question of what you like, Arthur," she is Arctic in her veins now. "He has high moral standards and you need to travel with a man of high moral standards. I suggest you go to Moscow."

"The realm of ice," I smile.

"What does that mean?"

"It's cold. Moscow is always icy, as Napoleon discovered"

And then, as has often happened to me, I become scared. I look at the two feet of my body. I don't understand how I dare defy her. I forget my resolution and say what I should have said a few minutes earlier "I know I have offended you, mama. Forgive me."

"Don't play act with me, Arthur. I see inside your soul."

"Why don't you come with us, mamma? We had such fun on the Nile. It will be splendid. And who, mamma, has higher moral standards than you?"

"You always speak cleverly, Arthur. It does not fool me."

I can hear the words she doesn't say. She deserved better. My father deserved better. When we decided not to have you smothered at birth, it wasn't so you would be obscene with Fanny Irvine.

"You leave in a week. You may go now. You can walk. You could have walked with those iron legs if you had wanted."

"They were too heavy," I remind her.

"You didn't try. I said you can go now."

She knows I hate the waddle walk on my stumps. I make it to the door. If you stand two foot high and you no have arms, you can't even reach the door handles.

I can't leave the room. We stand there – furious mother, furious child.

I will not beg her to open the door for me.

"I said you can go now, Arthur."

"I can't open the door."

"Remember that, Arthur. You can't open the door, you can't wash yourself, you can't pull your trousers down. You can do nothing by yourself. Don't forget that."

She strides out through the other door at the other end of the room.

Into exile

Arthur tried many different tactics to persuade his mother not to send him away. He suggested he would do useful work on the estate where the Famine was still raging. Arthur wrote to Boxwell pleading with him to intervene. But Lady Harriett had no intention of letting Arthur delay his departure. Arthur had to atone for his sins, sins that were too dreadful for her to spell out – even to him. She did not come to Dublin to say goodbye to the son she had once doted on. When they left Borris, she only told Arthur that she hoped he would return a better man. She had had doubts about his character when he had given up on the iron legs and now, he had disappointed her even more. He did not even get a kiss from her.

And we don't even know if Arthur managed to sneak away to say goodbye to the mysterious Fanny.

Chapter 5

The teenage traveller on an epic journey

Lady Harriett decided Tom Kavanagh should accompany his younger brother into exile. Both young men were put in the charge of the Reverend Wood who disapproved of Arthur. Lady Harriett was certain she could count on Wood. Her patronage could make a vital difference to his career and he had no intention of disappointing her. Lady Harriett made one point very clear, she did not want Arthur to return to Ireland too soon. He had to learn his lesson. She gave Wood a sealed letter which she ordered, was to be given to Arthur at a good moment, when it might make Arthur think about how he had misbehaved. She told Wood the gist of the letter. Lady Harriett trusted him more than she did her son and so set up a clash between Arthur and his tutor, a clash which was to dog the whole journey.

As he travelled, Arthur's letters to Lady Harriett were usually tactful and cool. In his journal, Arthur often recorded arguments with Wood but he did not complain to his mother about 'The Parson', as he called him. Wood, on the other hand, believed part of his job was to write to Lady Harriett, the truth, the unflattering truth and, sometimes, more than the truth about Arthur.

Between 1848 and 1851, Lady Harriett continued her travels. She knew much of the journey she sent her sons was dangerous. Two British missionaries had been killed a few months before Arthur, Tom and Wood passed through Central Asia. Yet Lady Harriett never suggested she was worried about the safety of her sons or that they should consider returning. She had become obsessed with the need to teach Arthur a lesson he would never forget. Lady Harriett's letters to Arthur, Tom and Wood never hint that she misses her sons.

This is an unflattering picture of Lady Harriett but one incident reveals how arrogant and detached she could be now that she was fifty. In 1850, Queen Victoria went to visit Dublin. It was the first time a reigning monarch had been to Ireland for decades. Unusually, Lady Harriett was in Borris at the time. All Ireland turned out to greet the Queen, all Ireland except for Lady Harriett. She confided to Wood that "I have neither curiosity nor loyalty enough to go to the expense and trouble of being presented to her myself."

But, then, Queen Victoria had not attended the ball of the century, on the eve of the Battle of Waterloo.

Arthur's journal records the hardships, dangers and the not infrequent pleasures of the voyage. His judgements are often brash. He seems to have forgotten the lesson of Jerusalem in 1847, that sometimes, the natives and the infidels are more civilised than the white man. The main defect of the locals from Lapland to Persia, Arthur noted, is simple; most of them are not English gentlemen. They lie, grovel, cheat and, also cook very badly so that he had to endure gastronomic disasters from the Arctic to the Arabian Sea.

Arthur was no travel writer. He and his companions were among the first Europeans to reach Kurdistan, but he manages to say little about its people. Even when he arrives at exotic locations like Baghdad or Persepolis, he says virtually nothing about them in his journal.

Horrid breakfasts in Sweden

The journey started with bureaucratic difficulties. Arthur had problems in getting a passport but, finally, on June 14 1849 the party sailed from Ireland for Copenhagen. By July they had reached Frederikshaven on the Baltic. Arthur's first entry in his journal concerns drink. In Denmark, the booze, at least, was good. They had the best porter and wine they had had for some time so "whether we enjoyed ill gotten goods we did not care to ask."

Things got worse further north. On July 8, they sailed to Stockholm where the Ambassador, Sir Thomas Cartwright, was "cold and uncivil" to them. They also had the misery of "a beastly supper and bad beds". Arthur did not think there was much to see in Stockholm, so they headed north to Uppsala. The food was no better there; they had a "horrid breakfast" and the "wine was abominable." They returned to Stockholm, but when they left the city on July 18th, Arthur delivered a sharp thumbs down. He left "the beautiful but stupid city of Stockholm with no regret."

On July 25th, they arrived in Cronstadt. Again, they had to spend a number of days sorting out their papers to travel on to Moscow. But on July 30th they took a diligence to Moscow.

Moscow did not impress Arthur any more than Stockholm had. He had expected the Kremlin to look more antique – an extraordinary remark given that the palace dated back to the 15th century. St Basil's Cathedral, with its domes like scoops of ice cream, gleamed in what we now know as Red Square. Wood insisted that they tour Moscow's many palaces but, even he became bored with one historic marvel after another. It was people rather than the architecture that made the greatest impression on Arthur. "We saw a group of prisoners facing a march of 5 months on the way to Siberia." Their grim look moved him. They were suffering and, he realised, would suffer more.

Ironically, given Arthur's bitching about unscrupulous foreigners, it was an Englishman who gave the young men the first serious trouble. The man was called Murchison and he had a French lover, Mademoiselle Dupont. Arthur, Tom and Wood worried the pair had put together "a most villainous scheme to cheat us of 100 silver roubles ... a more bare faced liar than Murchison I never met," Arthur sniped.

Unfortunately, Arthur's journal does not explain the swindle that Murchison and Dupont attempted but it made the Kavanaghs and Wood so furious revenge was necessary. One day the three young Britons and their servants were outside the house where Dupont lived. She was angry they had failed to con the young men and she did not act like a lady. She "gave us a shower of very dirty liquid out of a very dirty utensil." Raining slops down on the heirs of the kings of Leinster was not wise. The Kavanagh blood was up and, for once, Wood was with them.

The young men kicked down Dupont's door. Arthur stood guard while Tom, William, two other servants and the Rev Wood ransacked Dupont's house and pummelled Murchison. The noise was frightful; Dupont's neighbours ran to get help. Arthur was on guard as sentry and, when he spotted some of Dupont's friends running in to rescue and "I gave a warning to the best of my ability. It was too late." Dupont's friends attacked the Britons. There was "a desperate scrimmage", and the staircase in the house was "pulled down". The police finally arrived and were bribed not to arrest the young toffs. Still, Arthur's party decided it might be sensible to get out of Moscow for a few days.

The next day they headed for Vladimir about 30 miles from Moscow. The town was famous for its bazaar where one could buy skins of all kinds of beasts, including polar bears and polecats. Arthur also hoped to meet some Chinese merchants for the simple reason that he had never met a Chinaman before.

It was Tom who first got restless and started to say it was time to go home. But it was less than three months since they had left Ireland and Wood knew Lady Harriett wanted them to be away for much longer. He suggested that they visit Nijni Novgorod, which was famous for its monasteries and churches. Tom agreed but he was not very enthusiastic. Once they reached the city, the group bickered again. Wood wanted to visit every church but Arthur refused. He rode around the town with William and they met more interesting company – gypsies and gypsy girls. Wood was outraged.

Tom seems not to have enjoyed Nijni, however and wrote home to say he had had enough of travelling. Arthur worried that Lady Harriett might let Tom return which would mean he would have to travel alone with Wood. Arthur begged Tom not to go home and reminded him of how furious their mother would be if they came home without permission. He had seen how chilling she could become.

In the end, the young men agreed to play a game of billiards to decide "whether Tom should go home or come with us to India." Wood won the game "And so the fate of our journey was changed." Arthur wrote. They sealed the bargain with a bottle of champagne. Moscow had nothing more to offer, they

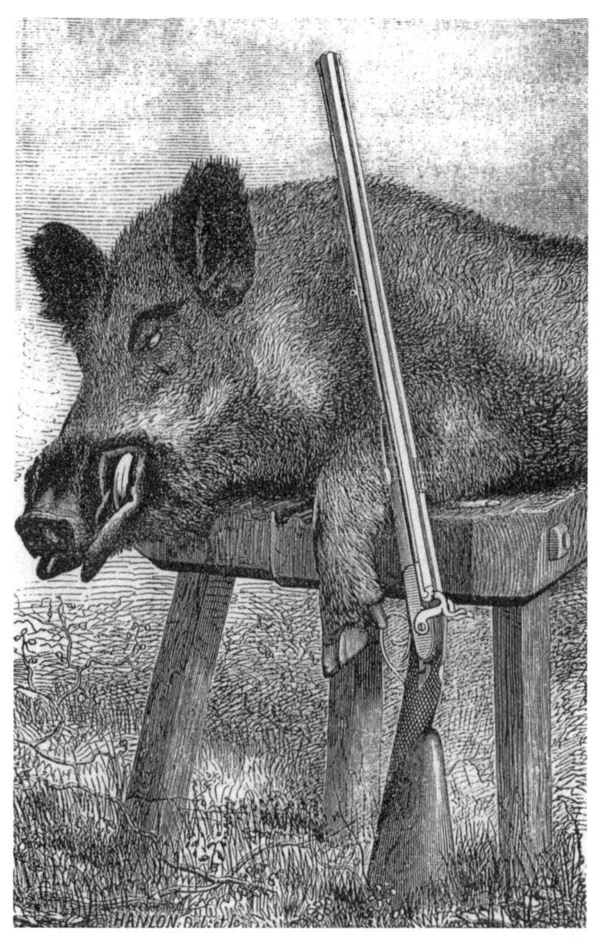

Sarah Steele included this picture of one of Arthur's prizes in her memoir of 1891.

decided, and so they booked on a boat that would sail down the Volga. Their destination was Astrakhan, roughly 840 miles away at the northern end of the Caspian Sea. They would cross Persia and take a boat to India. Arthur wanted to hunt tigers – and India was the best tiger country in the world. They were very young and they did not realise they were setting out on an epic and dangerous journey.

They sailed on the S.S *Hercules* which had room for fifty passengers. The Parson was being a pest as usual and wanted a cabin to himself. Wood complained when he had to share with

Tom. Then, the cooking on board was awful. On September 8, dinner "consisted of what the cook termed chicken but it was so tough it must have been Noah's cock." It's hard to imagine Arthur didn't intend the pun.

It was not all rock hard poultry, however. On September 14 and 15, as the ship sailed down the Volga, they saw flocks of ducks, geese, and wigeon. Arthur itched to shoot them but they were too far away on the wide river. The Volga was taking them into lands the Tsar ruled but where the culture was increasingly "Mussulman", as Arthur called it. On September 25, the ship docked at Astrakhan on the Caspian Sea. The next day, they sailed on for Baku at the southern end of the sea. The travellers got out some bottles of brandy and shared them with the crew. Everyone got drunk and Arthur was sick by the time they reached Baku.

The three young men had to smarten themselves up to visit the governor of the city. He took them to see the naphtha gas fires that provided Baku with light and heat. They seemed to have been in an unusual hurry to leave, however. After just two days, they headed south for Teheran. Everyone warned them the road was very dangerous. Bandits roamed the mountain passes. It was no place for Europeans. But Tom, Arthur and Wood were in no mood to wait.

Almost as soon as they left Baku, they got into a fight. One of Arthur's dogs killed a chicken "which occasioned not a little stir." The young men were pelted "diligently" with rotten eggs and bad oranges and had to ride away quickly. They then passed a village where they were offered the Bible and prayer books that had been looted from two British missionaries who had been killed. They thought it prudent to buy the books.

The travellers were not prepared for the coming winter weather. Between Baku and Teheran lay mountains that were hard to wind your way. The roads were just dirt tracks, the wind beat down, it was getting colder and colder. Even though he was a good rider, Arthur found himself in real danger on the mountain tracks. On 17 October, his horse was hugging a path zigzagging along the side of a mountain when "twice my horse slipped and one of his hind feet was over the side." Arthur was helpless. Belted into his saddle, he was trapped. His horse teetered on the edge of the precipice.

Arthur couldn't jump to safety. Just as when Bunny had fallen, he was stuck to his horse.

His horse tottered again: "If he had not recovered himself I would have been dashed into 1000 pieces," Arthur wrote.

It was now, just after Arthur had faced death, that Wood chose to reveal to Arthur Lady Harriett's letter. Wood seems to have positively relished this duty. Lady Harriett had not just been scandalised by his behaviour towards Fanny Irvine but also by his lack of respect for his mother who felt she had no control over him now that his father was dead. She told Arthur that she was worried about "allowing you unchecked to rush into a wild vortex of idle and extravagant pleasures with no father to guide or control you and a mother's voice too weak to be regarded."

Arthur knew he had to reply.

Arthur's diary

As I sit in the tent, freezing cold, I know that what I am struggling to write is sincere and, also, not sincere. I don't like to admit my feelings for my mother now are not entirely loving. I know I should forgive and forget but I remember too many things. Maybe if you don't have arms and legs you have a memory like an elephant.

As I write, I remember her ice in the veins stare when those bloody metal legs collapsed under me.

I remember her leaving me when I was eight years old.

I remember waiting for the post hoping it would bring letters from her for me.

I remember crying when I realised she had not bothered to write.

I remember deciding I wouldn't cry any more. I was eight.

I remember writing so many letters. Always the same question. When are you coming back, Mamma? Always the same plea. Please come back, Mamma, I miss you so much.

The Parson smiles at me from the entrance flap of the tent. "Writing are you?'

"Yes."

"Shall I arrange for it to be sent?"

"I'll give it to William." I don't want Wood reading it. I know the tone my mother expects – the humble sinner imploring forgiveness. I write:

> *Dear Mamma,*
>
> *For what has happened I can only say that I am sincerely sorry. Please do not take this as a hypocritical apology to induce you to take me home . . . it is simply that after having heard it and thought so long on such a thing, I thought the least I could do was to write to you to tell you how sorry I was for what had happened.*
>
> *As for my returning home or going further. I am perfectly ready and willing, of course, to do whatever you wish me.*

Wood stands above me. Smiling. "You wouldn't be writing to those gypsy girls? That wouldn't be why you want William rather than me to send them."

"Most gypsy girls can't read," I say.

"You know them better than I do, of course," he leers.

The road to Teheran

The party finally reached Teheran on October 25. It had taken four weeks to travel about 300 miles. After four months on the road Arthur was exhausted and needed nursing. He felt seedy, he wrote, and ran a high fever. For the next ten days, he lay in bed. Neither Wood nor Tom took much notice. They insisted on leaving Teheran before Arthur had recovered fully. He was too weak to argue.

On November 10, Wood again insisted they had to leave for Mosul. They had no immediate reason to. William was also sick. To head off was a stupid, stubborn decision; but Wood was adamant. Arthur wrote it was a journey of 8 days "the misery of which I can only remember, some days being barely able to sit on my horse." The bitter cold affected them all, but especially William. He developed frostbite and lost a finger. By November 16 William told Arthur they would have to bury him where they were. He just could not carry on.

But Arthur and the others refused to abandon him. So, William had to be physically helped every step of the way. They reached Mosul two days later and hurried to find a doctor. The diagnosis was alarming. William was in danger of losing all his toes to frostbite. As William was his personal servant, Arthur could make a decision without reference to Wood. He decided to send William back on reasonable roads via Trebizond and Constantinople. Arthur hated it if anyone other than William had to perform those intimate tasks – like wiping him – which he just could not do for himself but he was afraid William would not survive.

When William set off for home, Arthur had to hire a replacement but there was not a great deal of choice. The man they chose – who we only know as Pierre from Arthur's journal – turned out to be a mistake. He tended to make fun of Arthur and he was always wheedling for tips.

Though Arthur was unwell, Wood did not show much compassion. When eventually, he wrote to Lady Harriett to say that Arthur was feeling better, he added that had not improved his character. The Parson sniped, "but there is only one thing we have to fear – that he should not over eat himself. I continually preach self denial to him, although he received my lectures with some impatience." Arthur knew his mother would pay no attention to anything critical he said of Wood so he seems to have persuaded Tom to stir up trouble. Lady Harriett must have been astonished to get a letter from Tom in which he said that the puritanical Wood was "hopping about the ballrooms with Georgian women, his hair all dyed."

Arthur dismissed Pierre and hired a new servant, a rather gloomy German, John. John did not demand tips or make snide remarks and he was able to speak some Farsi, which was a help, but he could not replace William. In his journal Arthur complained of loneliness. Tom and Wood did not take much notice. They visited Tiflis without him as he still felt so seedy.

Ironically, while he was alone in Mosul, Arthur made an important new friend – and one of the few "Mussulmans" who won his respect. On December 15, Arthur breakfasted with Prince Malichus Mirza, the son of a pasha Arthur called "Fat Ali Shah." Prince Mirza had known the great traveller Richard Burton who introduced the *Kama Sutra* to the West. Mirza liked Arthur and admired his courage.

With Tom and Wood gone, Arthur complained "I spent the most miserable Xmas." The Prince must have realised how unhappy Arthur was because, on January 2, he made Arthur a remarkable offer. The Prince suggested the young man come to stay in his harem. The servant John was not, of course, allowed in. Arthur accepted and on January 3. he entered Prince Mirza's palace. It may be that the Prince assumed that Arthur was a eunuch though Arthur's deep voice was nothing like that of the castrati. In the harem, the Prince gave him into the care of an old female black slave. She took him to his rooms.

That first day, Arthur was still very unwell. But the Prince sent him a girl Arthur referred to only as "the beautiful Armenian". In his journal, Arthur wrote that "she awoke in me the deepest compassion by her longing for home."

When Wood returned from Tiflis and discovered where Arthur was lodged, he went into a puritan frenzy. Over-eating was bad enough but he had never imagined his pupil would worm his way into a harem. Wood rushed to the local missionaries but they had no intention of offending the local Prince. Tom who had a good sense of humour found the situation funny, especially when The Parson kept sending letters into the harem begging Arthur to leave at once. His soul was in peril and his mother would be informed. But Arthur was having far too interesting a time to listen.

Apart from saying he met a beautiful Armenian girl and that he recovered from his fever, Arthur did not write anything in the journal about his experiences in the harem. The facts emerged some ten years when he spoke of his time in the harem to Henry Labouchère, the radical M.P.

Arthur's diary: the wonders of the harem January 1850

I do not wish to be rescued from the harem, as Wood suggests. My soul is not in peril. I am given a splendid room with a couch and a small table. Tapestries with intricate designs are draped over many of the walls, rugs woven with fine traces of colour are scattered on the floor. The smell of incense and perfume is intense. They burn rose and lavender and other flowers and herbs in a brazier. It's a perfumed palace.

The black slave deposits me on the ottoman in my quarters. She smiles "chai"

"Tea," I smile, "thank you."

I am still feeling feverish but it is not the black slave who returns with the tea. A young red haired woman opens the door. She carries a tray with a silver teapot and a dish with pink and yellow Turkish delight.

She stares at me. I have often seen that stare. Horror, pity, what the hell do I do next, because is this creature human? She recovers herself well.

"Pauvre petit," she smiles. "Vous parlez français?"

"Oui."

"Vous voulez un peu de thé," she has striking green eyes. She pours some tea into a cup and, then, stops. She has realised I cannot hold the cup.

"Permettez," she says. She brings the cup up to my lips.

I drink some of the tea and am careful not to touch her hands. I presume only the Prince can touch the women here. "Très bon," I smile.

She sets the cup down. She stares at my face.

"Le Prince est absent. Personne ne vas entrer ici," she whispers.

She kneels beside me. "Vous devez souffrir tellement."

I tell her the truth. I don't suffer except when I think. I dream of, but do not know, what it might be like to be normal. I say I learned long ago to find ways of dealing with some of the physical problems. I do not want her pity.

She stands up and turns herself away from me. Slowly, she unbuttons her chemise. She lets me see her beautiful, big breasts.

"Mais sans mains vous ne pouvez pas les caresser," she grins.

I may have no hands, I say, but I can caress her breasts with my lips.

She laughs, surprised. I laugh too. She understands, as the girls in Ireland had understood. She picks me up. She holds me away from her breast. She can decide whether, when to bring me close to her brown nipples. She waits.

"Permettez," I say.

She laughs, again, and folds me to her breast. I start to kiss her nipples.

"Pas si vite, mon petit," she whispers. The harem has eyes, ears, footsteps, secret viewing holes. She puts me down on the ottoman, gets up, locks the door. She comes back and sits down by me on the ottoman. She wraps me in her arms.

"Permettez," she strokes me on my bum.

She sighs when I kiss her nipples.

After a few minutes, she undoes the buttons of my trousers. I tell her I rely on my servant to carry out such intimate tasks. She says that Ireland must be strange if I have to rely on a man to unbutton me.

She looks at me. I have seen that look before, the relief when she sees I am normal between my no legs. She cups her hand round my lance. Nothing missing, all correct and erect. She likes or maybe she has been taught to give pleasure.

It has been over four months – since the gypsy girls – that I have made love to a girl.

Afterwards, we lie back on the cushions and she tells me she is from Armenia. Her father sold her to the Prince when she was only twelve. The Prince realised she was intelligent and taught her to read. Together they studied the Kama Sutra. She asks me if I have read this book. When I say I have not, she promises to explain its basic, and very practical, philosophy to me.

During the rest of my stay, I am always afraid that the Prince would find us but she tells me not to be so anxious. In fact my only problem is The Parson. Wood bombards me with long letters of the sort he imagines the Archbishop of Canterbury would write. Have I gone mad and abandoned God? Have I turned Turk? My mother will be disgusted I am in the harem. She refused to enter the harem in Constantinople to stay with the Pasha's wife. I reply I would hardly abuse the Prince's hospitality by monkeying with his concubines. I add I am still feverish. I make my handwriting a little shaky to prove the point.

After ten days, the Prince re-appears. He is jovial and asks if I am better or whether it is a torture to be in such a heathen palace where they do not have Christian virtues. He smiles conspiratorially and says. "I know . . ."

"Your Highness knows what," I reply nervously.

"That you are really a man. I have watched . . . there is a secret spy hole. You have enjoyed the Armenian who is enjoyable. I have enjoyed you enjoying her. I was with another woman. Or two. We are men. Women exist for our delight."

Not a very Christian view, I point out.

"You yourself have not been acting in a manner the Pope or the bishops or the Rev Wood would think of as very Christian, unless the Kama Sutra is one of the books of your Bible which I haven't read."

Honour is everything for the Mussulmans. I have insulted him by making love to his woman. I am afraid he will never let me out alive.

"You are right . . . Normally I would kill a man who had dared make love to one of my women. But you are different. You are a marvel not even imagined in the Kama Sutra."

He explains the Armenian likes me because for the only time in life she has power over a man. In our love making, I could not hold her down or force her. I was at her mercy and she found that erotic. He found it erotic to see her so abandoned. He watched me, heir to the kings of Leinster, fucking. I should be outraged but I find I cannot be.

"I'm talking to you as I would to Burton," he explains, "as I talked to Burton after he had become educated in our ways."

He says that I am welcome to stay longer. I am tempted. I imagine telling Wood I have decided to stay in the harem. I imagine the letters he would write to my mother.

"You will make the Armenian cry if you leave. We learn in the Kama Sutra that if you meet a worthy man then to share a woman with him is no shame."

I smile, thinking how The Parson would respond to this Eastern philosophy. I offer the Prince a good price to allow the Armenian to return to her people.

"I will share her but I will not sell her," the Prince says.

"And you won't let her go."

"If she left here, she would be ruined. A woman who leaves the harem is not a woman a decent man will marry. She would become a common whore."

"What happens when she gets old?"

"She will live here comfortably. I won't send her out to starve."

My Armenian is very dignified when she comes that afternoon. She sighs. I don't desire her any more. I'm like all the other men, heartless. The fact that I suffer doesn't make me kinder. She had thought I was different. I try to nuzzle her, to comfort her. I tell her I have never been so moved by any woman.

She turns her back on me and walks out.

I leave the harem ashamed of myself. The old black servant carries me to the entrance of the Prince's palace where Wood and Tom wait for me.

"I hope you have recovered," Tom smiles mischievously.

"I am in better health now"

The Parson picks me up roughly. "I shall write to your mother about this debauchery," he snarls in my ear. He shakes me.

You can put me down, Wood, I say. But Wood isn't listening.

The Prince is shocked by his behaviour. "Mr Arthur has been my honoured guest," the Prince insists. "He has done nothing you Christians should be ashamed of."

"How would your Highness know what makes us ashamed," Wood snaps.

"I thank you for looking after my brother," says Tom diplomatically. He takes me from Wood and hands me over to my servant, John. I tell John I want to move closer to the Prince.

The Prince kisses me on both cheeks. "If I had a son like you, I would be very proud."

Proud of what? Wood shouts. We know what goes on in there, Wood adds. He is beside himself.

The Prince walks away from us.

"So what were the girls like," Tom asks. This is one of those days when he is more with me than with Wood.

"I have already written to Lady Harriett explaining your disgraceful behaviour," Wood says.

"In a harem, only the master may speak to the girls. I only saw the elderly slaves."

"You have seen things no Christian man should see," Wood spits.

"How would you know, Parson, because you have no idea what I have seen."

"I can imagine. The fact that I am devout doesn't mean I have no imagination."

It is one of the few interesting things Wood has ever said. He storms ahead of us back to our lodgings. That night after dinner, he asks me whether I want to pray. He is amazed when I say that I do. He has no idea, as we kneel, that I am not praying to atone for what he thinks of as my sins. I'm praying for the body and soul of my Armenian, asking her to forgive me, asking God to forgive me for having abandoned her in her unhappiness. If the Prince really desired her, he would not have let me share her. There are women in that harem he loves far more – and she knows that because once she was his favourite.

Early travellers to Kurdistan

The Reverend Wood insisted they leave Mosul, city of unspeakable sins, as soon as possible. In mid-winter, the road to Urumiah was bitterly cold but, at least, they were better prepared than they had been in November. "We owed our lives to our Russian coats and 4 bottles of Arak," Arthur noted.

On January 29 they reached Urumiah. The town was famous for its gardens and it overlooked a huge lake. As usual, Wood made contact with the local missionaries. They were Americans and so devout they did not serve alcohol "which I thought rather a bad plan in such cold weather," Arthur wrote. He liked the fact that the missionaries were exotic. "They said prayers in Syriac and they were introduced to two Nestorian bishops."

Arthur wanted to stay in Urumiah till it stopped snowing hard but, again, Wood would not hear of it. So they set out on what would prove to be the most dangerous part of their journey, the road into what we now know as Kurdistan. It was truly an undiscovered country at the time.

On February 20 it was so cold their clothes froze. The mules could hardly walk. Their only food was one cooked chicken and some bread, not much to share between six of them. However, they still had three bottles of port, and they needed the comfort of alcohol. When they got through the mountains, it became warmer and Arthur found "my clothes were also thawing. I had to undergo a trial of the watercure."

On February 21, there were huge snowfalls into the river, which made it too rough to travel by boat so they had to dismount and pull the mules. After 7 hours of backbreaking work, they found a cave to shelter in.

On February 23, they finally set out across the pass of Riyak. Arthur had an original theory for their survival. "I expect we owed our whole skins to our poverty, possessing little more than our horses, our rifles and a change of clothes – one shirt on, one shirt off."

The bedraggled travellers were very glad when they found what seemed to be comfortable inn in Riyak. They slept soundly but when they wanted to leave the next day, the landlord "locked the house and refused to open it till we paid a large sum of money. We refused and drawing our pistols told the landlord if he didn't open it at once we would blow his brains out." The landlord assumed the English milords were haggling. He would take half the sum he had originally wanted. But Arthur and his party were fuming now and one of them put a pistol to the landlord's head who "saw we were in earnest, which decided the matter." The journal does not state if they got away with paying nothing or just a reduced charge. But the locals got some revenge, stealing a servant's coat and Tom's rifle.

On March 1 1850, they reached Mosul again and then travelled down the Tigris on a raft made of goatskins. They reached Baghdad on March 22. The city housed a number of European missions and the three young men were made very welcome. They led "a very merry life between balls and dinner". During their stay, they went on an expedition to nearby Kayeroum where they bought a very nice little mare. Master Jack made fierce love to her kicking all the horses that presumed to look at her.

The British Resident said that if they wanted to see Babylon they should go now which they did. Arthur said only that the ruins were splendid. By March 30 they crossed what Arthur called the old woman's pass which they were told was the most dangerous in all Persia. The horses often had no footing but Jack, Arthur said, "carried me over with only two falls more than any of the horses with nothing on their backs could boast of." It was warmer now and they could sleep out in the open or on the roof and admire the night sky. They went to Shiraz and Persepolis though Arthur said nothing about these visits in his journal. In Persepolis, Arthur had another bad attack of fever.

Their wanderings over the next few months suggest they weren't clear what to do next. They were almost killing time while Lady Harriett decided whether Arthur should be allowed home.

After five months in Iraq and Persia, Arthur had become thoroughly disenchanted. He detested the flatteries, the salamaleks (literally, "peace be with you") and "the rotten compliments and never ending lies are enough to disgust any man who lays claim however small to common sense." Travel had not softened his prejudices. On May 7 on the way to Ishafan, they met a large number of locals who were fleeing. They had heard their Khan was on the way and they wanted "to avoid being plundered." Further on, the travellers met a Bactum chief "who came to scrounge wine for which he had a very un Mussul-manly predilection. I feigned sleep in order to avoid being bothered." On May 18 Arthur refused rather rudely to come and eat with the Khan. Tom and Wood had to apologise but Arthur was in no mood for politeness. He told Wood. "I begged his Reverence to save himself the trouble on my account as I did not care a d- for all the dignitaries in Persia." (He obviously meant "damn".) He sniped the Khan "travelled in a small caleche of which an English farmer might be ashamed" and that the so-called prince was "surrounded by fools and blackguards."

The next day when they passed the Khan's camp, the situation got worse. A servant came out and stole a dog who, as Arthur saw it, belonged to him, but the servant also claimed it was his dog. "I, of course, refused to give him up as I had bought him. We both got fierce and, I believe, rather scurrilous." Arthur had to appeal to the Khan. As in Jerusalem in 1847, it was the uncivilised heathen who found a diplomatic solution. The Khan said the dog was his property but gave it as a gift to Arthur.

On June 26th, they finally reached Teheran. Unfortunately, Arthur's journal then has no entries until the end of the year. In November, Tom and Arthur decided they could not bear another winter in Persia. But Wood was still afraid of defying Lady Harriett. There were a number of arguments again but, this time, Wood did not get his way. Tom and Arthur insisted they go down to Bushira on the Persian Gulf. If they could not return to Ireland, they could go further East. They booked on a boat for India. Arthur was perhaps the keenest. He had less and less hope that his mother would let him come back to Borris. He had been exiled, he had lost his mother's love, the two men he had been closest to – Boxwell and William – were thousands of miles away and he had no idea if he would ever see them again. But he could at least fulfil one of his ambitions and go hunting tigers.

The ship on which the young men sailed for Bombay was packed. Half was partitioned to take the harem of a local sheikh, but this time Arthur got no privileges. Yet again, the cooking was dreadful. The choice was "starving or masticating the patriarchal cocks on board."

On December 28 1850 they arrived in Muscat. They reached Bombay a week later where they put up at Hope Hall Hotel. Ironically, now that they were back in the British Empire, the travellers faced their first real financial crisis. Tom's letter of credit was withdrawn and, without it, they could not get money at the bank. Usually, a letter of credit would only be invalidated if instructions to that effect had been given in Britain. The young men had not asked Lady Harriett if they could go to India. The obvious explanation for the credit problem was that she instructed the bank not to advance any more money to Tom or Arthur because her children had defied her.

"We found ourselves in rather a doubtful situation, the bankers considering us swindlers," Arthur noted but he was exaggerating. The Kavanaghs were a great Irish family. Sir Edgar Percy, one of the directors of the East India Company, agreed to act as Tom's security while the situation with the letter of credit was sorted out. It was just confusion, Sir Edgar was sure. Wood wrote to Lady Harriett explaining the awkward position and, he wanted to wait in Bombay for her answer but Arthur had no intention of letting the wildlife escape him. "My mouth was watering for a fine old buck," he wrote.

And there was considerable choice of species to shoot. In his *Big Game Shooting in India*, Stockley detailed some 53 species of game, ranging from Himalayan ibex to the snow leopard to the elephant, lion and tiger. All were there to be gunned down.

At first Arthur planned to go hunting with a certain Captain Romaine but the Captain changed his mind, sold his horses and went off to Calcutta. Arthur feared "that the expedition would have to be given up". He was surprised when Wood suddenly became enthusiastic about big game hunting as he had never before shown the slightest interest in shooting. Arthur hated the idea of going with Wood, but he hated the idea of giving up on the tigers even more. He agreed to go with Wood but he couldn't help being ironic about The Parson. Wood, Arthur mocked, "made tremendous preparations for killing game, getting enough bullets moulded to shoot all the tigers in India and also getting a boar spear, his reasons for which I could not make out as he seemed to find it difficult enough to sit on his horse without any encumbrance."

On January 20 1851, they set off from Bombay with 15 "flunkies" and crossed the Poona railroad. They stopped at Tannah where Arthur was overjoyed to discover a bathroom in the Travellers' Bungalow. But it was not all luxury. Arthur wrote, "There I had an encounter with a tremendous rat in the bag shop which I killed with Wood's spear." Arthur wielded the spear just as he wielded a gun, held between his rib cage and his arm stump.

The party reached Kandala on January 23. Here Arthur ran into a man he had seen earlier in Poona and recorded one of those extraordinary stiff upper lip colonial encounters that the British Empire was so proud of. According to Arthur, Stanley and Livingstone should never have spoken to each other because they had not been formally introduced at their club. In Kandala, Arthur and the man from Poona were – "whistling tunes for each other's edification we did not speak because we were not introduced." Arthur waxed lyrical on "how proud Englishmen should be of their customs that bars all social intercourse between travellers who may chance to meet", and where "the slightest deviation from the letter of the law would be considered a most outrageous breach of manners." So the two pukka sahibs whistled and went their separate ways. In their pith helmets I like to think.

Arthur's first experience of hunting with native trackers was dismal. One native guide scared off the deer. Then, Arthur's party lost their tents and "we were obliged to throw overcoats over our horses and fastening the reins round our waists we did our best to go to sleep."

On February 18, they finally discussed where they might look for tigers. A week later, they started their adventure. Arthur sometimes rode on a horse and sometimes on an elephant. It took a few days to reach tiger country.

Finally, however, Arthur saw what he had longed to see – a tiger. "We espied his Majesty, that is the tiger, lying between a large rock and mimosa bush but before we could fire, he gave a loud woof and dashed down the valley exposing himself to a fire from the hill." But the tiger took shelter in an almost impenetrable jungle of wild prickly pear bushes.

They rolled large stones to shift the tiger. When they had forced him out of the bushes, they chased him. The tiger roared; the white man aimed. But Arthur missed with both his bullets. The tiger turned to face his enemy. Death stared Arthur in the eye. He did not panic.

"I then took a pot shot at him and was fortunate enough to send my ball behind his left ear. He retreated." A few moments later, Arthur had the tiger in his sights 50 yards ahead. Arthur's third bullet wounded him badly. "The tiger rolled helplessly about into a bush about 5 yards from where we stood. We gave him the contents of our rifle and polished him off."

He was a fine young tiger, Arthur noted.

After this exciting chase, they returned to camp. They had to sleep in the open again and Arthur now developed an unpleasant boil on his backside. For much of the next 10 days they hunted, even though Arthur's boil hurt badly. But the chance of killing game always made him feel less depressed. He even cheered up when three hyaenas came to drink near where he was half-sleeping. They made so much noise he woke up and shot at them. He bagged one and his mood lifted at once.

Six days later, the "flunkies" had news of another tiger. The party

Bombay Green around 1850, with horses.

roamed the countryside but could not find him. The hunters became impatient so they employed dangerous methods to force the tiger into the open. "In beating the jungle, crackers were used which set fire to the dry grass and in a moment, the whole hill was in flames ... we had quite enough to do to get the elephants out in time," Arthur wrote.

Five days after the fire, they had better luck. Arthur found himself head to head with a tigress and shot a bullet through her eye. He bagged another tigress a few days later. By June, Arthur had shot two more tigers. His remarkable exploits began to be talked about in Bombay, which turned out to be extremely useful in the next few months.

When they returned to Bombay, Tom fell very ill with what seemed to be consumption. The letter of credit situation was still not resolved. A doctor suggested Tom needed to escape to a different climate. It would have been reasonable for the group to return to Ireland. But Wood was still haunted by Lady Harriett's orders so he suggested to Tom that they sail for Australia where the climate would help restore him. The Parson borrowed the money to pay for the tickets from Sir Edgar Percy.

Arthur now made an astonishing decision. He decided to stay in India on his own. He was sure Wood and Tom could manage and so in July he saw Tom and Wood off as they sailed for Australia.

Arthur now had to make a living until his mother relented and sent more funds. His exploits as a hunter helped. Sir Edgar Percy found him work in the District Surveyor's office in Poona. The District Surveyor mapped the countryside and planned roads and new buildings for the East India Company. For the first time in his life, Arthur felt he was doing something useful.

Arthur repeatedly wrote to his mother explaining his predicament. He also wrote to his brother Charley who was now the master of Borris, but his family seemed to have no interest in helping him out. He began to wonder if he would ever go back home.

We tend to think that journeys change an individual. We grow through adventures and experiences that test us. Biographers are always on the look out for turning points when their subjects change and you can map a new direction for them. Yet as I read

Arthur's journal, I am more struck by the ways in which this remarkable journey – an extraordinary achievement for a limbless young man – did not change some of his attitudes. He was still inclined to dismiss foreigners as dodgy dagoes even though many had been kind to him. He still compared their salamaleks unfavourably to the stiff upper lip. If one seeks changes, one has to be more psychological and I want to return to the theories of Erik Erikson.

Erikson stresses that the child has to learn to separate from the parent before he or she can become his own person. Disabled children need their parents even more than other children do. Only Mummy and Daddy can feed you, clean you, and love you. Some disabled children also sense that they are a burden and disappointment to their parents. Arthur had now been away from his mother and from his faithful servant William for a long, long time. He hadn't crumbled or died. He had learned to live on his own, among strangers. He had learned something few men of his class ever had to do – to make an ordinary living. He was, as he turned twenty-one, a remarkably independent and resourceful young man.

And, then, everything changed. Arthur was working on plans for a warehouse at Poona when a telegram arrived from Malaysia. Arthur wasn't expecting any news from Wood. He tore it open and he could not believe what he read. Wood and Tom had never reached Australia. Almost as soon as they sailed, Tom had become weaker and weaker and, after two months, he had died of consumption at sea.

Arthur was beside himself. He felt guilty he had let Tom sail with Wood. It confirmed his worst suspicions about The Parson. Arthur didn't wait to get permission from Lady Harriett. He resigned his job at once and asked Sir Edgar Percy to lend him the price of a ticket to sail back to Europe at once. Percy obliged and wrote to Lady Harriett himself explaining the tragedy that had befallen her son.

Arthur reckoned the quickest way home was to land at Suez, take the train to Alexandria and then the first ship bound for London. He wrote to Borris to explain the route he was taking back. The journey to Egypt was miserable. When he landed there, he found a letter from his mother at the shipping office. She still did not want him to head straight back for Ireland. He was to meet her at Corfu.

Reunion in Corfu

It was a tense reunion. Lady Harriett looked drawn and much older. She blamed herself because she had relied on Wood not just to teach her son a lesson but, also, to keep them both safe.

Arthur explained that The Parson had been very frightened of returning to Ireland without Lady Harriett's express permission.

That was true, Lady Harriett admitted. She felt it would only be decent to let plenty of time elapse till Arthur returned.

All he did, Arthur explained, was to kiss Fanny Irvine. He would always love and respect his Mamma but he pointed out that he was 21 years old – and that he had travelled more than most men with arms and legs. He could not be treated as a child any more.

Lady Harriett was offended. She did not think any son had the right to speak to his mother like that. God expected us to tell the truth.

"Tom died because of you, Arthur, he died because of your sins. God has really cursed the Kavanaghs. You are the one who should be dead. I do not know why God took my poor Tom . . ."

She was a lady. She couldn't pick him up and toss him overboard but she wanted to, Arthur felt. He minded, but not as desperately as he had done when he was a child.

Chapter 6

After the famine

As they sailed back to Ireland, Arthur and his mother found it hard to be really frank with each other. Lady Harriett was grief stricken and angry. She wanted to know why Arthur had not written about Tom's illness and why he had abandoned him when he was ill. Arthur did feel he had failed his brother but he also blamed his mother. After all, if she had sorted out the letters of credit for them, they would probably have left Bombay for Europe months before Tom fell ill. So Arthur and his mother were not able to console each other much.

Lady Harriett now turned even more to religion. God had punished them all by Tom's death. She was a difficult woman but, through her grief, she did realise that Arthur had changed. The trip had toughened him. She hoped that would not make problems at home. Her eldest son, Charley, was now the master of Borris but he was less self-confident than Arthur. She told Arthur he must defer to his elder brother; he must not try to out-fox him with his gift of the gab. Arthur still wanted his mother's love and he promised he would do just as she wanted.

Temperamentally, mother and son were utterly different and that became clear when they docked at Lisbon. Arthur went into the city, saw some monkeys for sale and bought two of them. Lady Harriett thought this was unseemly when Arthur was in mourning. She could not believe it when her son said the monkeys would cheer him up.

Lady Harriett constantly repeated that she expected Arthur to behave like a Christian gentleman on his return to Borris. Christian gentlemen did not pursue young women and, anyway, the hussy Fanny Irvine was now engaged. Hoddy had met her fiancé who was extremely handsome as well as 'normal'. Arthur told his mother that now he had no interest in the girl he had once thought of as his "dearest wife".

After a night in Dublin, they took the train back to Bagnalstown. The countryside looked bleak. It was raining and grey. The famine had left pockmarks, derelict buildings, beggars, neglected fields. The Kavanagh land agent, Charles Doyne, tried to make the return of Lady Harriett something of a celebration. The mistress was back. He gathered together some fifty tenants to meet her train at Bagnalstown. They cheered and she, gracious lady, acknowledged the applause that was her due.

In 1846, the Home Secretary, Sir James Graham wrote to the Prime Minister, Sir Robert Peel. "It is awful to observe how the Almighty humbles the Pride of Nations. The Sword, Pestilence and Famine are the instruments of his displeasure; the canker worm and the locust are his armies." Three million people in Ireland depended on potatoes for their foods, when the potatoes were blighted, they starved. The Irish Famine that raged between 1845 and 1850 was one of the holocausts of the 19th century. Tenants on the Kavanagh estate had suffered badly.

After the death of Lady Harriett's father, the Earl of Clancarty, the estate was run by the land agent, Doyne. Historians often criticise the role of the agents in the troubles of Ireland and many writers stress agents often were harsher than the landlords. Doyne knew the Kavanagh family and its foibles well. His father had been the agent for Thomas Kavanagh. Lady Harriett had no sympathy for the tenants. They were lazy, backward, superstitious and they should not be allowed to avoid paying rents just because of the famine.

As Arthur arrived at Borris, he was struck by the house. It looked magnificent in the twilight, dim, mysterious, its turrets as of old. William carried Arthur through the grand living room and up the staircase to his old bedroom.

Arthur had always been interested in the estate and Tom's death made him feel he should assume more responsibility than he had ever done before. He had also learned a great deal working in the District Surveyor's office. And his attitudes were very different to those of the rest of his family. As he rode around the estate, Arthur saw the all too evident signs of neglect and decay. He rode to

Mullins, he rode to Ballyraggett, and he rode everywhere. The ravages of the famine had marked the whole area and Arthur wanted to help do something to make things better.

Today, historians speak of post-famine Ireland and argue the country suffered a collective post-traumatic shock but, as the 1840s ended, rural life was changing and many landlords did not like it.

Arthur was more sympathetic to the tenants' plight. He discovered Doyne was hated not just because of his evictions and unwillingness to compromise over rents, but because he mocked the existence of the famine itself. If the Irish hadn't been so feckless, they'd have coped. If there had been a famine in Sussex, no one would have turned into it a tragedy. Doyne was not exceptional. Some English papers carped the only reason there was a famine was that the Irish only worked two days a week. Doyne told Arthur he despised so many tenants because they lied.

Arthur had a sense of rank and he expected more respect from Doyne but he knew the agent could be dangerous. Arthur's diary hints Doyne made it clear he knew about the girls Arthur seduced and that it was always in his power to let Lady Harriett find out the truth. But there was no need for that to happen as long as Arthur did not make trouble by criticising the way he ran the estate.

When Lady Harriett discovered Arthur was away riding for hours again, it worried her. She suspected he was misbehaving again.

Arthur's diary: January 1852

My mother reminds me of our conversation on the ship. Fanny Irvine's marriage has been announced in the Times.

"I have no intention of making myself ridiculous, Mamma." I reassure her.

"You may have to face the fact, Arthur, that marriage is not for you."

I don't snap at the unspoken. If I marry, I may father cripples. The curse of the Kavanaghs will echo down the ages.

"Like all younger sons, you don't offer much to a girl of a good family," my mother smiles. My predicament is normal, for once.

I have travelled half the globe, survived disease, bandits, imams, salaams and managed to feed myself for a year when my mother refused all pleas for money but she does not say one kind word. If I ever have children I will praise them if they deserve praise, comfort them if they need comfort and never ice in the veins them.

I don't show a thing. I put on the bravado, the hopeful cripple. "Perhaps someone will fall in love with me," I say.

There is a long pause. "She would have to be an exceptional young woman," my mother says, "though I have always been a romantic at heart. One could not have danced on the eve of the Battle of Waterloo and not be that. I will always know what you are doing, Arthur. Mothers can see into the souls of their sons."

The silence prolongs itself. "I will go riding, mother," I eventually say, flatly.

The first girl I visit is Mary O'Callaghan. It's obvious that her family have suffered in the famine. Her mother has died. Her dress is shabbier than any dress I have ever seen her wear. She's thinner too though she still has fine breasts under her blouse. She lifts me out of the saddle.

"I'm a married woman now." She carries me inside the house and smiles a little shyly. I have brought her some chocolates. She opens the box and eats two. "I haven't had chocolate for a long time." She breaks into a big smile. "Well, you wouldn't marry me would you, Arthur?"

"I'd have liked to see my Mamma's face if I tried," I grin.

"Mistress of Borris ... I knew how to play with you but I'd have never been good with a fish knife or telling the butler where to put Lady High and Mighty at dinner ..."

"I'd like to give you and your husband a wedding present,"

"Thank you," she says rather formally.

"I will send you twenty pounds. I've always liked you very much."

"I'd like to say we don't need your money but Patrick, my husband, is in debt. Doyne keeps putting up my father's rent even though half the potatoes are black."

"And if you won't pay?"

"He tells us there are hundreds who'd be happy to pay the rents."

"I'll put a stop to that."

"Are you master of Borris? I think not. Your brother lets Doyne do what he wants."

"I want to know everything he's been doing."

"You have become the serious young man," she laughs.

"I have travelled to the ends of the earth. It shakes you up."

"Was it dangerous?"

"Once or twice." She looks intently at me and then, she touches my face.

"I shall miss flirting with you," I say.

"Flirting?"

"I wouldn't use the other word to a respectable married woman."

I want to kiss her. I haven't kissed a girl since I met my mother on Corfu. Ice in her veins Mamma has eyes in the back of her head and spies in her pocket. William tells me how much she gives him to report on my sins. Mary and I are both greedy. She wants more chocolate and I want her.

"I'm married now and I love my husband." She picks me up in her arms and takes me out to the horse. She gives me a kiss on the cheek. "We're all very glad you are back safe," she says.

Conflicts with Charley

Lady Harriett was not the only person who blamed Arthur for the death of Tom. Charley who had become an army officer also felt that Arthur should not have allowed a sick Tom to sail off to Australia. In the evenings when he was at Borris in the summer of 1851 Charley wanted to hear everything about the adventures of the young men. Arthur, on the other hand, wanted to talk about the famine, how it affected the estate and what might be done to improve the situation. These were not topics that interested Charley much who was perfectly happy to leave the running of the estate to Doyne. The last thing Charley wanted was for his brother to interfere, especially as Arthur kept on saying that the family had a responsibility "to our people".

"I've sworn an Oath to Her Majesty – not to the bloody peasants." Charley said.

Arthur also could not help but notice that Charley had started drinking a great deal, and when Charley was drunk he would get quite belligerent. The adventure that fascinated Charley above all others was that of the harem. He wanted to know what the girls were like and, of course, what Arthur had got up to. Arthur gave him a rather limited account; it would only be to Henry Labouchere that he would tell the truth.

When Arthur would not oblige, Charley reminded him of the realities. Arthur was not to interfere. He, Charles Kavanagh, was the lord of Borris. He pitied Arthur, of course, who could never be a soldier and he knew that his brother always wanted to be doing things. But he did not want people laughing at his brother. If as lord of Borris, he and Lady Harriett were content to leave the business of the estate to Doyne, Arthur should keep his nose out of it. Charley added that he was happy Arthur was back and happy for him to spend his days riding and shooting and fishing.

Often Charley stomped out of the room after these encounters. Arthur would be left alone and distressed. He wanted his mother and his brothers to love and respect him.

Arthur's diary

I pull the bell cord with my mouth to summon William. When he arrives, I tell William to have a horse ready. He is used to strapping me in the saddle at the strangest of hours. I ask him to place my silver-topped stick in the sheath in my saddle.

Dark is falling as I gallop out of the drive. A slim moon is rising, a crescent moon, the moon of the Mussulmans I have seen all over Asia. I would like to go and make love to Mary but she will not have me now. I turn for Ballyraggett. Dr Boxwell has moved back into the district from Dublin and bought a large house just outside the town. Being known as the Kavanaghs' doctor is good for trade. Boxwell welcomes me at his door and embraces me. I tell him I have just quarrelled with my one living brother.

"Your brother drinks too much whisky."

"Is it Tom's death?"

"I don't know," he puts his arm round my shoulders.

"While you've been gone Arthur I've developed a new hobby. It's just what you need when you're unhappy." He carries me into his large garden and sits me in a large chair. He tells his gardener to light torches. He goes into the shed and returns with two axes. "This is the perfect cure for you. Axing ... it's good exercise ... it sweats out the shit ..."

"But I can't hold an axe."

"If you can shoot, you can axe." Boxwell puts the handle of the axe between my right stump and my shoulder.

The first time I try, the axe slips.

"Try again," Boxwell picks the axe up and places it back between the stump and shoulder. I tighten the stumps and swing again. I thump the wood. It's pure pleasure.

"You'll get the knack of hitting the same groove."

Boxwell watches me as I swing and hit, swing and hit. He mops the sweat off my brow.

"Mr Gladstone, the new Chancellor is a great axe man," says Boxwell. "An hour of this and it's hard to be angry with anyone."

I swing the axe again.

"Your brother will not listen. It suits him to have Doyne run everything because he lacks the will power to run the estate. Charley dreams of being Wellington, of beating Napoleon. He hopes that if he becomes a great soldier, your mother will be happy."

"She would be," I say too sharply.

"I've been a doctor long enough to realise he suffers from melancholy. There's no cure. It comes, it goes. I suspect your brother tries to fight it sometimes by taking opium."

"When we travelled, we smoked it sometimes. It does make you feel less seedy for a little."

"It warps you because you can't do without it. I despise opium," Boxwell says passionately. It's one of the things I like about him. He is passionate for, passionate against.

We resume axing. After an hour I am utterly exhausted. Boxwell wants me to stay the night. As a doctor he would have no difficulty in attending to my needs, he assures me. But I hate anyone other than William doing these inevitable things. Boxwell straps me into the saddle that he designed and I gallop out into the road. The silver-sliver moon is low in the sky. Owls make that strange hoot. I love this land.

I tell William to take me up to the corridor where Charley's rooms are. Brothers should scrap but not quarrel deeply and we have quarrelled deeply. I must make it so we are friends again. I'm not sure what to do. The house is silent. I tell William to go. I grasp the silver stick between my stump and my shoulder and knock for my brother.

"I'd like to talk to you, Charley," I say. There is no answer.

"Why won't you talk to me," I say again.

Charley won't answer. I sit down at my brother's door. Tom is dead. Charley will not talk with me. I knock again. I feel a fool in the silence. I heave myself up on to my pathetic stumps and waddle down the dark corridors. I want to cry but I don't. The servants must never see that.

The curse of the Kavanaghs

Arthur decided that the best way to influence Charley was to flatter him and remind him that their father had taken a very personal interest in the estate. Arthur also suggested to Lady Harriett that he should make himself useful and persuaded his family to let him work as an under manager for the estate. It was an interesting moment. Irish agriculture was changing dramatically after the famine. By 1859 50% less land was devoted to arable farming than ten years earlier. The number of cattle, on the other hand, increased from 3 to 4 million. Progressives and traditionalists debated the best ways to make farms thrive again. Though he was politically conservative, when it came to farming, Arthur's instinct was always to be progressive, to use the latest techniques of scientific agriculture. He introduced horse-drawn reaping machines into Carlow, for example, but every new idea met opposition from Doyne.

Arthur established a busy routine for himself. He was always up early and started his day with shooting in the deer park. William would carry him to the wall of the park. Arthur would press his body against the wall and, standing on his tiny leg stumps, he would shoot a deer and have it brought back to the kitchens.

After a hearty breakfast, Arthur would ride round the estate. He drew on his experience in the district surveyor's office at Poona and made many plans to better the estate but he did not have the power to insist they were carried out. But, he talked to Doyne constantly and almost lobbied for changes.

As the under manager of the great estate as well as a Kavanagh, Arthur was in social demand and he liked that. In 1853 he acted as a steward for the first time at the Carlow races. Inevitably, many of the daughters of the tenants found it flattering when he made it obvious that he would enjoy making love to them so Arthur continued to have not very meaningful affairs with girls on the estate.

Arthur received visitors and business colleagues wearing a cloak. It didn't disguise his condition, of course, but the cloak made him look respectable. But he often became irritated at being stuck in his armchair. If he wanted to get closer to someone, he would slide off the chair and "hop" towards them. He hated the word "hop" but it described his movement accurately.

Whenever Charley came back from the Hussars, there was always the risk of a quarrel – and Arthur hated that. The loss of their brother should have brought them closer but it did not. Charley continued to drink heavily. It was a complete surprise to Arthur when Charley announced he was going to get married. He would resign his commission with the Hussars and take charge of Borris like his father had done.

The preparations for the wedding were advanced when tragedy struck again. A month before the wedding, Charley went to bed with a cold. He wrapped himself in a cloak and started to drink whisky. He lit a cigarette. No one was ever sure if what happened next was a terrible accident or a deliberate act. The cloak caught fire. Charley spilled some alcohol on the cloak and it started to burn furiously. He did not get to the bell cord to summon the servants. No one heard screams or cries for help. No one smelled burning until the fire in the bedroom was out of control.

Finally, the alarm was raised. Servants rushed to Charley's bedroom. They knocked the door down. They made a chain with buckets of water and they did manage to put the fire out. But it was too late. Charley Kavanagh was dead; Arthur had lost a second brother.

Arthur feared Charley had committed suicide. Boxwell tried to comfort him. He pointed out that usually suicides left a letter behind. There was no letter. It would have been infinitely less painful for Charley to shoot himself, Boxwell said, and that suggested it was not suicide but an accident.

Charley had not even left a will. Yet again, it was left to Arthur to send Lady Harriett the dreadful news. She began to feel the family was really cursed.

The only one of her sons alive was the one who, in the usual course of events, would have been smothered at birth. But she did have her faith and this was a moment for faith. God must have designed Arthur for some purpose though she could not see what it possibly might have been. She got back to Ireland in three days to bury her eldest son. It was a desperately sad funeral. And for Arthur it was the decisive turning point. Arthur liked Shakespeare and he knew he had had "greatness thrust upon him." He also knew that his mother doubted he was fit to be the master of Borris, the greatness he had inherited against all odds.

The new lord of Borris

After the funeral, Arthur established what would become a life-long routine. He woke early and went out riding. He promised himself he would protect his inheritance with all the strength and cunning he could muster.

He rode for a week round the estate. He slept in different villages and sent William back for supplies when he needed them. Having talked to many tenants, he summoned Doyne.

The land agent acknowledged that they had had many disagreements but he also knew that Lady Harriett would back him in any dispute with her son, so he was hardly nervous.

Doyne was taken aback when Arthur started to list the many complaints tenants had of the way he had run the estate. Arthur added his own observations on how Doyne neglected some of the property because he did not want to invest money. Doyne became more and more agitated.

"I shall honour my family's obligations to you Mr Doyne," Arthur declared in a grand voice in the grand drawing room, "but this estate will now be run on scientific lines and with justice. If you can help me do that, I shall be glad to continue to employ you as my agent."

Doyne conceded that Arthur had always had interesting ideas but pointed out that he had been away from Ireland for many years. Doyne was no longer talking to a poor younger son but to the master of Borris, and what Arthur wanted to know was whether Doyne would help him achieve his ambitions.

For the first time in his life Arthur had real power. He knew that if he dismissed Doyne the agent could find it hard to get a new job. Doyne agreed to let Borris' new lord become an active and innovative landlord.

Arthur's diary: re-union with Mary

On the Friday I ride to see Mary O'Callaghan. Now that I own Borris, I will reduce the rent she and her husband pay.

"If it isn't lord and master Arthur," she smiles. She is wearing a new blue dress and carries me into their cottage. It seems more cheerful than before.

"You used my wedding gift well."

"It was kind of you but I had to explain to Patrick. A marriage with secrets . . . isn't much of a marriage."

"Where's your husband?'

"Gone to Wexford to look for work." She makes me some tea, pours and brings the cup to my lips, smiles.

I am in a strange mood and the mood makes me too blunt. "I should love to kiss you," I say.

"I'm a married woman."

"I was just admiring what I've lost." I look up at her and bring my face close to hers.

"No, Arthur, I'm wearing a wedding ring."

"But not on your nose," I grin. The grin works.

We both laugh and the laugh became a rubbing of noses and the rubbing of noses turns into a kiss, like the kisses we used to have.

"You're in mourning, Arthur," she pulls away.

"Doesn't some poet say we die a little when we make love?'

I know she does not really want me. But she is a little afraid. I am the master now. Better give me what I want. She bargains though. She makes me promise this will be the last time. She closes the curtains and lies me down on the bed. She undresses me but she does not take off her dress. She slips out of her under-garments and she takes me inside. She knows I want to suck her nipples. She sighs but she lets me. I suck her nipples as I've done since we were fourteen. If you've got no limbs, your lips become strong and subtle. They are what you use to kiss, caress, lick, love. Mary knows that and she can't resist the sucking. Finally, she smiles, tosses her head and gasps and gasps.

Afterwards, she strokes my stumps. "I will go to confession and beg forgiveness and explain this was an act of mercy. Do you think the priest will let me get away with that?"

"I expect so," I say.

"And now, you better go. I will never let this happen again. You'll find plenty of girls to make love to. You're the master now. They'll tumble out of the trees for you."

"Why are you angry?'

"I've just betrayed my husband."

"You need to help me on my horse," I remind her. As soon as I am in the saddle, she turns back into her cottage. She is crying.

Three days later William tells me he has seen Mary bandaged and bleeding. His friends have told him her husband thrashed her when he found out I had gone to their cottage.

I realise I have to marry or there will be other disasters like this. I know I forced myself on Mary. I surprise myself and go to see my mother. I tell her that it is in my nature to want a wife. She understands what I mean. Now that I am master of Borris I have something to offer to a young woman of breeding.

You must not hope too high, my mother replies.

The marriage of Arthur Kavanagh

Lady Harriett's attitude did change quite abruptly partly because the family now needed him to produce an heir. The line of the Kavanaghs and the Le Poer Trenches must continue and Lady Harriett did have one possible bride in mind.

Frances Leathley was the daughter of a clergyman at Louth. She was distantly related to Arthur and had known him for many years. She admired his courage. Lady Harriett knew that Frances would not find it easy to marry as she had no dowry. When they met, Frances told Lady Harriett she was not sure she could marry Arthur. It was hard to say what she was really frightened of. If they had children, would she become the mother of monsters?

Lady Harriett was a persistent woman, however. She wrote to Frances often and slowly persuaded her that it was her Christian duty to marry Arthur. Lady Harriett cajoled the poor relative with some skill. She invited the Rev Lealthy to stay. She insisted that God must have a purpose for Arthur. Why else would he have survived when both his brothers had died?

Arthur liked Frances. She seemed intelligent and quiet. She had read the Scriptures attentively. For some months Frances resisted the pressure but, in the end, she accepted Arthur's proposal. Once she had done so, Lady Harriett said that it would be best never to speak of the fact that Arthur had no arms or legs. The very model of submissiveness, Frances agreed.

Lady Harriett felt that it would be grotesque for her son to have a society wedding so the marriage was a quiet affair at 1 Mountjoy Square in Dublin on March 15 1855. The vicar of Clongoose conducted the service. Arthur stood on a special chair so that he could be at the same height as his bride.

There was no need to be so shy at Borris. Everyone in the district knew Arthur's condition. After the honeymoon, early on March 27 1855, the tenants started to arrive, wearing their best clothes. Arthur met them at the gates of Borris and led people to meet the "graceful form of the future mistress of Borris." Arthur loved music and he had hired a band so that everyone could dance. Frances waltzed him round the hall in her arms. Arthur felt so relaxed, he even

Frances Kavanagh, Arthur's wife.

started to dance on his stumps. And the honeymoon had been happy.

Arthur's diary: Dublin, March 15 1855

I had been careful not to kiss Frances while we had been courting. I had booked the bridal suite at the Gresham Hotel in Dublin. It had two bathrooms, which was necessary for me.

Frances and I dine. She had wanted no company at all. I point out William always fed me.

"I will feed you, Arthur."

She sits by my side. We start with oysters and champagne. Frances holds a large succulent oyster to my lips and I suck it. It reminds me of the sex of women. It's not surprising just before our wedding night. Frances dabs me with a napkin and sucks an oyster out for herself. We sup slowly. After the oysters, there is turbot à la Marseillaise and a fine haunch of venison.

I suggest we have champagne brought up to our room. "But before we drink, my dear, I do need William."

William carries me into one of the bathrooms. I piss. I ask him to wash and towel my genitals, which he does without saying a word.

"Will that be all, Mr Arthur?"

"I think you should wrap me in a towel ..."

"Good luck, Mr Arthur"

"I don't need you to wish me luck,"

"I have wiped your arse since you were seven so I can wish you luck on your wedding night." He puts me, wrapped in the towel, on the bed. I feel like a box of chocolates again.

"I expect you'll be telling the bride about the harem," he laughs.

I hope Frances has not heard a word of that exchange. She walks out of her bathroom in a simple white night shirt.

I smile at her. "Fran, I wish I had arms I could wrap round you."

"Your mother said never to mention the fact you don't have any."

"We shan't live together well if we ignore the truth."

She sits down on the bed and puts out a hand on my face.

"I suppose if you had arms and legs it would be easier ... And

I've never, of course, been close to a man. I don't suppose you have been close to a woman as . . ."

"As I've no arms or legs"

"I was going to say as you're a Christian," she smiles.

"Once or twice on my travels, Fran, in lands which are not Christian I did things which perhaps were less Christian than one might wish. I may not have arms or legs but the rest of me is perfectly normal."

Under the towel, my prick is rising. A little more of this and it will be sticking up like a tower in a towel. It does. Frances stares at the protuberance.

"I would love to be able to take off your clothes . . . it's what lovers do."

"Do you want me to take off my clothes?"

"It is our wedding night"

She steps out of the nightdress. She has lovely pert breasts with dark nipples. She stands shyly in front of me.

"You're very beautiful," I say.

She blushes. I realise she has no idea what to do next. She also assumes that I have no idea what we should do.

"Why don't you place your breast against my mouth?"

"Is that what wives do?" I have surprised her.

"Among other things."

She does not expect the feeling when I start to suck her nipples. She claps her hand to her mouth in panic.

"No one can hear us, Fran, moan, groan, gasp. Make as much noise as you like."

The towel has fallen off. She stares at my prick.

"My mother died when I was twelve, Arthur. I think mothers usually tell their daughters what happens on the wedding night."

"In the Bible it says that sex between man and wife is good. God gave it to us not just to have children but also to enjoy. It's not dirty or strange or, for that matter, very complicated."

I play with my tongue on her nipples. She gasps. For a moment I think of the Armenian and a gypsy girl in Nijni and Mary but they disappear from my mind and I see only Fran. She isn't plain at all.

"You have made love to other women," Fran says.

I am delighted I have not married a fool.

"I will never make love to another woman now that you are my wife."

She is amazed by the pleasure she has felt.

"It can hurt girls the first time. If I had a hand I would put it between your legs"

"Like this," she puts her hand between her legs. "I read the Song of Songs last night because I know it mentions breasts and ... but not ..."

"The word is cunt."

"Cunt. It rhymes with runt."

"It's not a word to use at dinner parties," I say.

"I don't remember father using it in any of his sermons."

Then suddenly, without my asking, she puts her hand on my prick. I gasp with pleasure and turn my body to face her. I kiss her wildly.

"Don't you ever dare do this to anyone else," Fran smiles when we have finished kissing.

"I thought you were meek."

"If you're a clergyman's daughter and poor you have to play meek. I'm not meek and you're not a virgin."

We're pleased by what we have just discovered – that we can tell each other the truth. My prick is a pink rock.

"There's a very rude word for what we're doing. Fucking,"

"It rhymes with sucking," she says. "If this is fucking, Arthur, why do women complain so much about it?"

I have found a wonderful wife.

Becoming a father

It was not just in the privacy of the bedroom that Frances turned out to be surprising. She persuaded her husband to give her a handsome allowance of £110 a month. Within weeks, she announced she was pregnant. Frances then started to suggest to Arthur that they needed their privacy. There could only be one mistress at Borris. Lady Harriett was simply too domineering. Lady Harriett knew the Victorian conventions. There could only be one mistress in a house and, now, Frances was the mistress of Borris.

Arthur arranged for his mother to take over the Georgian lodge in Ballyraggett. Lady Harriett liked the house, which still has a magnificent staircase, but she hated leaving Borris. It was a kind of defeat.

The prospect of becoming a father terrified Arthur. He worried his children would have his deformities. Lady Harriett could not hide her fear of that either. Boxwell was, as always, his best ally. He reminded him that he had always believed Arthur lost his limbs because of a freak in the womb as the umbilical cord strangled his arms and legs. Freaks did not repeat themselves. Despite everyone trying to reassure her, Frances was frightened. She and Arthur prayed a great deal together and Arthur smoked more and more.

The couple celebrated their first New Year together in 1856. A fortnight later, Frances went into labour at Borris. Arthur smoked in the living room. He tossed about on the sofas desperate for news. Boxwell and the midwife sent one of the servants down with news regularly. It seemed to be going fine. Then, Boxwell rushed into the room at 3.30 on the afternoon of January 14th 1856. It was the best news. Boxwell told Arthur his son was fine. The baby who would be christened Walter was healthy and perfectly normal. Arthur cried for joy. Boxwell smiled and carried Arthur up to see his beautiful son and heir. The curse of the Kavanaghs had been defeated.

The village celebrated as soon as the news was out. Torches were lit that night. The single bell of the Catholic Church rang. Tar barrels were set alight in the streets.

Arthur was to prove a loving and very involved father by the standards of the age. He took great interest in the education of all his children and spent a great deal of time with them. Having a child proved to Arthur that he could have a normal life. He threw himself into the life of Carlow with huge energy. He planned a programme of that word he came to love "improvements". In Ballyraggett, Arthur offered free timber and slate to those tenants who wanted to improve their cottages and farm buildings. He organised the building of limekilns in the area. He brimmed with confidence.

Arthur was not that happy with Doyne but he was loyal. The compromise was to hire a second agent called Bookey to help.

Arthur also re-designed houses in Ballyraggett village and was especially proud of his slate-roofed cottage, a design that won him the Dublin Society medal for architectural design. It's a tribute to Arthur's skill that some of the cottages are still standing.

When he became the master of Borris, Arthur joined the very pinnacle of Anglo-Irish society. It was estimated that 50 Irish landowners owned 80% of Ireland's land. Many of these landowners were happy to collect the rents and live lives of idle luxury but Arthur was too restless to do that. He also wanted to show that he could follow in his father's footsteps. He started to angle for the positions in the county that came almost automatically with his estate. His father had sat on the local bench as a magistrate and now Arthur got himself invited to join the bench. He was also invited to join the board of the poor house by Mr Sweetman, a large tenant who had once brought a court case against Doyne. A year later Arthur wanted to be named as the Chairman of the New Ross Board, which dealt with the poor in the area. Sweetman was worried he would be defeated in that ambition but, somehow, Arthur managed to get the post.

On January 1 1857 Arthur took a ride round his lands; he was inspecting, as usual, restless as usual. After the New Year was celebrated, Arthur resumed his busy routine. He was landlord, farmer, magistrate, overseer of the poor. On January 7, he heard the complaint of Father Doyle against a local doctor. Five days later Arthur went to Waterford because he was worried about the insurance for the estate. From Waterford, he had to go to Dublin. He had come to realise that the links between Carlow and Dublin were too slow and he started to campaign for a better railway.

By the end of the month Arthur was back at Borris. He was busy but he was not always well. Between February 26 and 29, he missed dinner because he felt "seedy". Arthur saw axing as one answer to his depression. His diary often mentions the trees he cut down. Boxwell was his companion often. "Out punting before breakfast. Axing trees till luncheon. Finished off axing in the evening,", Arthur noted.

But the cures didn't always work. On March 13, which he noted in his diary was an "unlucky day though I don't really believe in it," Arthur did not leave his room at all. He had a headache and stayed in the smoking room rather than disturb Frances. He complained of insomnia and wrote that "I believe that between the 11th and 15th March I could not sleep at all." There were two reasons why Arthur was worried and they may well have contributed to his insomnia. First, he had money problems; second, Arthur's father had been an M.P. The next election was due to take place in April 1858. The local worthies would soon decide who would stand in the Tory interest for Carlow. Arthur wanted the nomination but he was afraid that he would be "subject to a defeat". Cripples did not sit at Westminster. Arthur's good friend John Sweetman thought there was a real risk of Arthur being humiliated. He was up against one of those "impossibles". And so Arthur became depressed and "seedy"; he had to make a real effort to work. But he did usually manage it.

On July 23 he took judges into the courthouse at Carlow and stayed listening or trying criminal cases till 4 p.m. On the next day he had a bad toothache. As well as axing, Arthur found sailing often made him feel better. In September he sailed from Waterford to the Needles. By the end of October he was back in Carlow and full of energy again. He organised a meeting for the relief of those who had suffered from the Indian Mutiny, which collected £240.

All the investments, which aimed to improve the estate, led Arthur into unexpected financial problems. He went to Dublin on November 2 because he had to consider something he hated, mortgaging some of his property. The end of the 1850s saw economic problems in Britain after the boom of the previous decade. Some banks failed, many railway companies went bankrupt. Arthur lost £2000 in the Johns Brothers smash, which was a major banking collapse.

Frances was pregnant again and the couple celebrated the birth of their second son on December 10. Frances set off to Dublin to find a wet nurse and once he was sure mother and baby were well, Arthur went off for four days sailing. He was back for Christmas, which he loved to celebrate at Borris. But this Christmas, he had a hard choice to make. While he was sailing he had realised there was an alternative to mortgaging the house. He could sell his yacht. If he also made some drastic economies in the running of the estate, he would not have to go begging to bankers. Arthur didn't hesitate.

He sold the yacht and made Borris financially safe. At the end of that year, he was pleased with himself. He had not had to place the property of the once kings of Leinster in hock. Once again he had survived.

Arthur Kavanagh in middle age.

Chapter 7

Hunting for a seat 1860–1864

By 1860, Arthur had established himself not just as a successful landlord but also as one of the leading personalities in the Carlow area. One of his eccentricities was amusing. He was a Justice of the Peace but he also got in the habit of holding an informal court beneath the great Oak Tree at Borris. One of the monkeys he had bought on his way back from India sometimes sat under the oak too. Arthur's tenants would come with complaints and requests and he would sit there, part wise, part enlightened despot, and dispense justice. People loved to hear him talk about his travels and his plans. Frances and he also led a busy social life. Arthur adored his wife – he had kept the promise of his wedding night and never thought of being unfaithful – and he enjoyed playing with his small sons. Walter, his heir, was 5 years old and Anthony was two.

His relationship with his mother was less straightforward. Lady Harriett still travelled a remarkable amount for a woman of sixty. Though she and Arthur were no longer at odds, they were not that close. Lady Harriett could still be very cold and cutting.

Arthur's depressions did not disappear as he settled into his life as a great landlord. On his 30th birthday, in 1861, Arthur observed bleakly "I know what it is impossible for me to have." He often had to remind himself of his many blessings. As he coped with more local responsibilities, Arthur began to dream what must have once seemed a ridiculous ambition. He had always wanted to follow in his father's footsteps and become the Member of Parliament for the area.

In the memoir she wrote, Arthur's cousin, Sarah Steele, insists Arthur did not even try to get the Conservative nomination for the seat of Carlow in 1862. Frances was sure he would hate being a Member of Parliament; he would be stuck in London for months. No hunting, no shooting, no fishing. He would be reduced to trotting a horse round Hyde Park.

Sarah Steele accepts this version as the absolute truth but, like much of the Victorian writing about Arthur, it does not quite convince. First, many M.Ps in the mid-19th century were country men and didn't give up riding, hunting or the country life just because they happened to sit in the House. The Commons worked less than 36 weeks in the year. It started business at two in the afternoon; few members attended every day.

There were real concerns though. Entering Parliament would mean huge practical problems for Arthur. The geography of the House of Commons with its winding staircases, crowded lobbies and long corridors was a nightmare for a disabled person. When Parliament had been rebuilt in 1834, lifts did not exist – Mr Otis patented his wonderful invention in the 1850s – and so Arthur would have to be carried up and down the different levels of the Palace of Westminster. He would be back to being a parcel or a box of chocolates. At home he could propel himself by "hopping" on his stumps but he could hardly do that in public.

The House was also a theatre, much as it is now. There is no evidence to suggest the basics of body language have changed in the last 140 years and some of that is reflected in the language we use. We say people have *stature*, literally that they are tall. In the 1860s, successful politicians dominated the House partly by their personal presence. In any public debate, we have to get attention to make a group listen to us. We jump to our feet. We put up our hands. We wave our arms. We get up to speak. We "display" to get noticed like an aggressive bird flapping its wings. It was much the same in the House. If you were a backbencher, you had to catch the eye of the Speaker to have a chance to speak. Then, you had to get up on your feet to make you speech. To make a point of order, you had to stand up and place a top hat on your head. A legless M.P. would have to speak sitting down. That was against the rules of the House.

In the 1860s, the procedures of the House also did not allow anyone other than MPs and officers of Parliament on the floor of the Chamber. Arthur could have had one of his servants carry him to the door of the Chamber or wheel his chair in. But what would he do then? Crawl? Make an exhibition of himself on his stumps?

Arthur also had other reasons for hesitating. He was conscious of his own lack of formal education. Greer's Academy was hardly Eton, Harrow or Westminster. In his journals Arthur let his feelings of inferiority slip out sometime. Once, when he and his party had landed 88 salmon in Norway, he reckoned that was not bad "for those who are used to unsophisticated Irish rivers." Arthur had seen many of the great rivers of the world – the Danube, the Nile, the Volga – but he made himself out to be a hick fisherman on a hick river. London was the most sophisticated city in the world. It is not surprising Arthur should have wondered if he could fit into that city's most powerful club, Parliament.

Yet Arthur felt the Carlow seat should have been his. He was not much of a democrat. For him it was a question of being the rightful heir. The head of the family had for three generations sat in the House of Commons. When he turned to his wife for advice, however, he found she was completely opposed. Frances was proud of her husband. When he had learned to ride, shoot and write, it had been a question of his will and patience. Arthur's social position had protected him from being treated the way the Victorians treated poor "freaks," but that might change, Frances feared. Standing for Parliament would mean asking the public to choose him rather than other candidates who looked, and who were, normal.

Lady Harriett also felt it was not appropriate for her son to aim so high. He should be content with his lot. He had married, he ran his estate. What more could he want? His mother could still provoke his insecurities.

In the end, Arthur did not dare seek the nomination in 1862. He did insist, however, on being the person who proposed the new Conservative candidate for adoption. The meeting would take place on his turf, where he had many friends who knew what he could do. In June, Arthur called the meeting to attention at Jury's Hotel. Then in his deep voice, he proposed Captain Beresford as their candidate. Captain Beresford was intelligent, he had fought for his country, he knew what worried local people. Arthur summed up the issues facing a new member, and then recommended Beresford. He added that if they had faith in Beresford, they should not bind him to vote in any particular way on any particular issue. He had to follow his conscience. It was a generous speech – but not one Arthur found it easy to make.

Once Beresford had been nominated, Arthur did not want to remain at Borris House and get too involved in the election campaign, however. To get over his disappointment, he planned a long trip abroad. The sea would be his consolation.

Having restored his finances in 1861, Arthur had fitted out a new yacht. On October 29 1862, he set out on the *Eva.* Sailing, he wrote, gave him time to think. Arthur wrote the only book he ever published about this cruise and it seems to me this was significant. In the book, he establishes a very definite persona – intelligent, humorous and very political. The text is entirely different from the journals of his trip to Moscow, Persia and Iran. This was no accident; Arthur wasn't writing just for fun. He planned to make an impression. He had decided to publish a book and the book was to be more than a record of local colour, hunting and shooting anecdotes. The notes are full of political comments for the book would prove – maybe first to himself – that he had it in him to become a politician and that, he deserved the Carlow seat.

At the start of the book, Arthur described himself as "the Admiral, Parson and Doctor" of the *Eva.* He took a crew of ten, four ladies including his wife and his sister and five dogs – Trap, Jeremiah, Snuffles, Carlo and Bob. "Our business in this boxing ourselves together with fourteen other living souls in the space of about 80 ft by 20 ft is what is described in Admiralty and Club rules as 'pleasure'." The pleasure, Arthur was frank, was "being bent on the destruction of all pigs, deer, woodcock, wildfowl or anything in the shape of game." The dogs were a nuisance at sea but needed "because finding game in the Albanian forests without their help is out of the question."

I have argued earlier that hunting became a passion for Arthur for two reasons. He could still shoot better than most men who had the usual arms and legs. It was a remarkable physical triumph and it's not surprising that hunting passionately helped him conquer

Arthur's yacht the R.M.S. Eva.

depression. Upset at not standing for Parliament, Arthur decided to take it out on the wildlife.

Hunting, Arthur always insisted, was a noble skill. "Many abuse it, calling it wholesale slaughter and murder," but that just betrayed their ignorance. He added it "is not such a simple matter as it may seem to make an effective shot into a large flock of wild fowl." One had to calculate the distance, the elevation and get the timing right. The trip would be a trial of skill.

We have seen that meals mattered to Arthur and the cook was the only member of the crew he described in detail. He was a person of "cadaverous leanness" and possibly psychopathic tendencies for his "soul delighted in twisting chicken's necks". Ashore, cook often got into fights but it was worth tolerating him as he could turn out excellent, if sometimes eccentric, meals which Arthur liked. "I have eaten camel in Arabia, horse in Tartary and poulet au champignons in Paris where I dare say I ate both cats and rats without knowing it." he boasted.

The *Eva* sailed and Arthur looked at the sea, and into himself. Being on the water washed away his anxieties, the nagging sense of his "impossibles". There is no more "thorough realisation of the word freedom than to be skimming over the boundless sea," he wrote.

The English Channel, however, was not very deserted, however. Boats, ships, steamers chuntered up, down and across it. "The steamers are the bête noires" because their captains often fell asleep at the wheel. "I don't want to be too hard on the chaps," Arthur joked. He was sure they didn't get enough sleep "but that's no satisfaction to the unfortunate fellow who is either run down or drowned by them." Arthur prided himself on always taking his turn at the watch and the *Eva* and her crew got through the Channel without hitting, or being hit, by another vessel.

Arthur's book never raises basic questions about how a disabled sailor can cope. The book states that Arthur, like every other man, kept watch. Could Arthur really be on watch alone? It would be dangerous for him to be the only person awake on the boat. He could not deal with a storm or a ship looming out of the mist on his own; if he fell overboard rather, as he had done years earlier on the Nile, he would drown quickly unless someone dived in after him. Throughout the book, however, Arthur never mentioned the everyday details of how he coped, of just how much he did alone and where he needed help.

The *Eva* reached Gibraltar on November 4th and they stayed there until November 15th. Arthur liked the Rock and gave tourists useful advice. The traveller could "call at old black Charley where you can easily get rid of loose cash by investing in slippers, scarves and other Moorish gee gaws." He recommended bars where one could listen to the local musicians and dance. Arthur loved music and loved to watch others dance. It's hard not to find that rather touching.

For the first time, however, Arthur wrote much about the strategic and political significance of the places he visited. The Rock was one of the rocks on which the Empire was founded. If Britain ever lost Gibraltar, the sun would be "setting on England," Arthur wrote. Gibraltar, Malta, Corfu should all remain British. The Med couldn't be a British lake, alas, but the more the Union Jack flew over it, the happier the natives would be. British outposts provided vital quarters "for our troops in the Mediterranean" and "safe good roadstead" for our fleet which needed "the heaviest gun practice."

After Gibraltar, the *Eva* set sail for Sicily. There was trouble with customs officers when they were leaving. Arthur sniped he had forgotten the golden rule of dealing with Customs officers, English, Irish or Turk. Bribe them. The problem was sorted out with a few gold sovereigns. After the baksheesh, the passage to Palermo was calm.

The bay of Palermo was one of the most beautiful in the Mediterranean, Arthur thought. They went sightseeing and had one unhappy experience. Their guides took them to a catacomb of "dried monks". The burial chamber stank terribly and he could not describe the vile smell properly "unless I were to give a chapter on chemistry." He added "I should rather be buried any day than hung up in a niche in a wall for a stranger to look at and most probably remark what an ugly sinner he must have been when he was alive." The stranger who looked at Arthur, dead or alive, would, of course, first notice his lack of limbs but he never mentioned that. This is the first of a number of passages that encourage the reader to assume there was nothing strange about Arthur's body.

Palermo prompted another set of political comments. Italy had just gone through its reunification. Arthur sniped about *libertà*. Freedom, he noted, had its drawbacks. "I am sure it is not a wholesome word when shouted by the *vox populi*. It has been and will be the excuse for many a bloody deed."

From Palermo, they sailed on November 24th to Naples, past Reggio and into Greek waters. Corfu was under British control. The nonsense poet and painter Edward Lear loved the place and was there at the same time. Arthur let his sense of humour out. He was amused by the look of some sheepdogs and thought he could read the canine minds. When the dogs stared at the chubby lambs, Arthur guessed they were thinking, "I should awfully like to eat you but I am in honour bound to defend you."

On Corfu, Arthur again considered history and politics. The British had imposed a Lord High Commissioner on the islanders and the Lord High Commissioner had caused offence. "The Greek Archbishop had not been invited by the Lord High Commissioner to a dinner party when his diocesans (or whatever you call them) considered that etiquette or respect should have secured to his

Grace a ticket for soup." The islanders were threatening to rebel. The P. G. Wodehouse tone doesn't mean that Arthur had no sympathy for the islanders. He conceded, "I am aware that their (the Ionians) national and proper pride was often wantonly insulted." He was also harsh about local landowners – a number of whom were British – who didn't realise property "has its duties as well as its rights". Yet he couldn't resist mocking the islanders with their 'dago' ways and sniping the Ionians could not really control their own affairs. If the Union Jack was forced out, the islanders "may yet regret the loss of that bit of bunting."

Sometimes, Arthur conceded the British took advantage of their power but he tended to dismiss that as mere high spirits. "I saw them once, bye the bye, put two shots nearly into the hull of a Greek steamer. Jack (by which he meant Jack Tar) is a mischievous lad by nature and was it not just 'nuts and apples to him' to see the unfortunate Greeks come round the point in range when he was showing how fast he could fire?" Sleepy captains in the Channel were irresponsible but trigger-happy tars, never – even if innocent Greeks got injured or even killed when "our" sailors larked about with cannons.

By December 17th, the travellers were ready to start hunting. For the next ten weeks, the *Eva* would sail up and down the coast of Albania, put in at small ports and, sometimes, return to the relative civilisation of Corfu. Arthur hired local men as guides and acquired more dogs. The hunters were mainly after pigs, though any game was fair game.

In earlier chapters I've described how Arthur hunted. In the Albanian forests, Arthur often either had to be carried by his men or to ride a pony. Again in the book he never mentions that he could not hunt on foot – or why that might be.

Once they had started hunting, only three things concerned Arthur – the animals and plants he saw, the thrill of the chase and the condition of the dogs. Arthur constantly worried about his failure to pot a sufficient number of pigs. On January 1st 1863, they were disappointed there was no woodcock. On the 2nd the all too wily pigs got the better of the dogs, butting them with their tusks.

After another week's hunting, the party returned briefly to the

One of the photographs Arthur took of Albanians who helped the party hunt.

island of Zante near Corfu. Frances and the three ladies stayed ashore while the men went back to hunt. Again, he flaunted his funny side. The ladies, Arthur said, were the perfect caricature of travellers who loved foreign parts but ... They had toured the island and found it enchanting though "they had been very nearly shaken to death" in the carriage. "The hotel was oh so charming but they did not like olives." A beastly party of men had made such a racket the delicate ladies had not been able to sleep. Such woes but "tiffin soon restored their serenity".

During the crossing from Zante back to Albania, Arthur decided it would be a good idea to practise what they would do if pirates confronted them. There had only been one recent incident of pirates daring to attack the British – the menace of the Barbary Corsairs had diminished after the British captured Algiers in the 1840s but Arthur liked the idea of gun practice. So they attached a bandbox to a buoy, let it drift away and took eighty shots at it.

They landed again in Albania on January 13. This time the pigs had lost some of their cunning and the dogs coped better. On the second day, however, Arthur nearly died. This is one of the only two points in his narrative where the attentive reader could work out there was something physically odd about him. "I was very near leaving my bones in Avalone as an offering to the pigs," he wrote, "for on the second day at Avalone my horse rolled over a precipice with me and only old Charley who was walking in front of me caught him by the head as he went over". Charley held the animal long enough to allow Arthur to get free and it was clear that if it had not been for his intervention, Arthur would have died. An attentive reader might stop to ask why the author couldn't get free by himself.

Frances saw what happened and gave a more dramatic account. "A small cactus bush, about ten feet below, checked his fall and Arthur quite calmly called to the sailors to unstrap him from the saddle." (Frances Kavanagh letters).

Arthur said he didn't suppose it would be a painful death falling 400 feet but when he looked down the precipice he started to shake with anxiety. He recovered quickly though. The next day he was riding over "a still more impracticable mountain" as energetically as ever, Frances noted, and the fall "did not shake Arthur's nerve in the least." He really was a brave man.

Some of the best hunting came at Petala, where between January 16th and 24th they killed 67 brace of woodcock, 33 brace of wigeon, as well as 2 brace of sea pheasants. "We would have been satisfied to have remained another 8 days" but the ladies were bored and bitched. They had to camp in the open. Everything stank. They heaped "a torrent of abuse" on Arthur who "saw impending signs of a heavy shower." Then, again he wrote one of those ambivalent phrases about his body; "stowing my tail between *my legs*, I gave it time to pass over." (My italics.) The phrase was no accident.

With the ladies complaining so much, Arthur agreed to leave Petala. As he feared the hunting got worse. They would spend another month after the pigs but he was beginning to feel gloomy about the insufficient amount of dead wildlife, his so-called "Bag".

Yet another harem

To make up for the awful conditions at Petala, the ladies planned a treat. They went ashore on an island governed by the Turks and were to be allowed to visit the Bey's harem. They never reached the harem, however, because they met a youth "his face a mass of pustules and scrobitic eruptions, excuse the nasty names, dear reader," but that was the truth. Petrified, Frances and her friends fled back to the *Eva*. Arthur was angry and his anger prompted another attack on the locals. The island's rulers had done nothing about the risk of infection. Rather "true to their fatalist creed they curled their fat persons on their divans, smoked their chiboukes and having repeated the only prayer (if it can be called prayer) that I believed a Mussulman knows – Allah il Allah – left the scourge to spread how it liked." The *Eva* left Plague Island at once.

On February 21st, back in Corfu, Arthur received worrying mail from Ireland. "Tenants were getting rusty," and "packets of hateful letters greeted my wakeful opticks – gloomy accounts from the Emerald Isle." But the next day they sailed back to Albania.

The night of February 22 nearly made up for all the disappointments about the Bag. Arthur was sleeping on the brow of a hill when he heard "a tremendous crashing. Sleep vanished in a second." Excited, he cocked both barrels of his rifle and gazed intently into the bushes. In the dark it was not clear what animals were making the noise. He had "visions of a right and left with 2 mighty boars biting the dust". But when he could finally make out the beasts, they turned out to be a herd of cows on the rampage – and gentlemen did not shoot cows.

On the trip, Arthur also practised another hobby – photography. He had acquired a good camera and plates. He would take landscapes or portraits of the natives. The book on the cruise of the *Eva* is illustrated with his fine coloured plates. They include a number of touching portraits of Albanian men and women and a big portrait of the crew. There is only one person missing in that portrait – Arthur himself. There is not a single picture of him on the expedition. He remained the invisible author. He was not going to let anyone see him as he really was.

Arthur's final act was to write up the log of every animal they had killed. On February 23, he totted up The Bag.

The bag

Pigs 10	Snipe 45
Deer 6	Plover 6
Jackals 6	Pigeons 24
Geese 13	Swan 1
Duck 54	Bittern 1
Wigeon 152	Sea Pheasant 7
Teal 100	Budgeter 3
Woodcock 203	Grebe Duck 4

The tally was not too bad, he decided, except for too few dead pigs.

As they sailed up the Bay of Biscay back towards Waterford, Arthur confided to his journal that he felt he was coming back from a school holiday. When he had been at school "the schoolmaster and tutors of younger days – disagreeable creatures they were – used to tell us vacations were given to make us return with refreshed minds and more cheerful attention to our lessons." The pep talk had not worked for him as a child and now "like a naughty schoolboy", he confessed he didn't relish going back to work in Ireland.

Arthur worked up the notes he had taken on the journey into a narrative for the book that presents a very definite persona. The author was a competent man, a good sailor, an excellent navigator – learned enough to discuss issues like why the compass does not point to true north – and a sharp commentator on recent political trends in Europe and how they affected British interests. He began and ended the book with politics giving his reflections on the state of Ireland. The trip had allowed him to escape from "post packs full of stupid wearisome letters . . . how I hate them with their bickering and jealousies or worse than that the curse of this wretched country – bigotry – displaying itself at every turn and from every side – everyone convinced that everyone else wants to convert the whole community to his plan of going to Heaven or elsewhere." Ireland's problems had not changed while he had been away but Arthur's comments reveal his basic attitudes. He loved Ireland but hated its religious divide – an enlightened position for his time and class.

In the book, Arthur comes across as an acute and witty, often self-deprecating observer. He is funny at the expense of easy targets – the fussy ladies, the weird foreigners – but he can also be funny about himself. He loves hunting but mocks his obsession with the Bag and admires the smart pigs that get the better of the dogs. The character that emerges is attractive in many ways. The only false notes are those ambivalent phrases, which gloss over how disabled he was.

Back in Ireland, Arthur was eager to get his notes into print. It seems reasonable to argue that he wanted to establish his credentials as a capable man, a man fit to be an M.P. before the next election.

Much would turn on how the story of the *Eva* was received. If the book were a failure, his family and friends would have been proved right. Parliament was no place for a pink torso. But if the book were well received, Arthur would have much more confidence in himself. A good reception would prove to him, he had a chance –

and the right – to take his place in the Commons. He might have no arms and no legs but that would not stop him being a big man on the big stage of national politics. The reviews were favourable; his friends also liked the book.

In 1864, Arthur went sailing for months again. This time the *Eva* went far north, to the north of Norway. The scenery was far more spectacular than in Albania. Arthur kept good notes of the wildlife they met including a number of whales but there was nothing of political interest to report on in Lappland. So while he kept meticulous notes about the scenery, animals and, as ever, about The Bag, Arthur did not work this material up for publication. He had no intention of becoming a travel writer. He had written the book to test the water and it had been well received. Arthur was quite subtle about letting people understand his new ambition. He did not want to risk rejection but he began to drop the odd hint, to recall his father's time as an M.P., to mention the investment he had already made in Carlow. Arthur no longer believed becoming an M.P. was one of his impossibles. If a seat were to become available, he was no longer too shy or too aware of his "impossibles" to fight for it.

Chapter 8

In the House

Early in 1866 the M.P. for Wexford was appointed a High Court Judge and had to give up his seat in the Commons. This time there was no battle for the nomination. Henry Bruen met with three other leading local Tories and they decided Arthur was the man they wanted.

A few days later, Arthur received them in the palatial drawing room at Borris beneath the domed blue ceiling. Bruen knew Arthur had been bruised by his experiences in 1862 when Beresford was chosen as the candidate for Carlow, and he was worried Arthur might refuse to stand. So he spoke first and he laid it on thick. All of them had every faith Arthur would make an excellent Member of Parliament. Arthur was pleased, more pleased than he let on to them but he felt he had to be careful not to seem overjoyed. Still, it was only polite to call for champagne and porter and to ask Frances to join them.

Arthur loved following in his father's footsteps. He knew enough history to be sure the Commons had never had a member who was "crippled". And that was the problem. He had never even visited Bruen in Parliament. He did not want to have to explain to the Serjeant at Arms the help he would need, the special permissions so that he could be boxed, basketed and carted through the lobbies and stairways.

In Queen Victoria's reign campaigns usually involved bribery, fraud and intimidation. In one way, however, Victorian elections were restrained. The press did not rake over the private lives or the health of candidates. If you were standing, you were a gentleman ... well probably. If Arthur's opponents questioned whether he was physically fit to be an M.P., they did so without leaving a trace on the record.

There were 106 Parliamentary seats in Ireland but 38 saw no contest in the 1865 election because one of the large landowners, or someone they backed, was returned unopposed. There were battles for the nomination in such seats sometimes. Comerford (1998) argues improbable deals were done between Protestant landlords and Catholic clergy. Post-Famine Ireland was still a deferential society. The priest and the grandee usually got their own way.

Wexford, however, had usually seen a fight. Arthur stood against the Liberal, Pope Hennessy. Arthur had the support of all the local grandees and many Catholics also admired him because he was a decent landlord. His Catholic tenants, he insisted, were treated just like his Protestant ones. The press divided on sectarian lines. The *Carlow Sentinel* argued Arthur would be an excellent M.P. and never raised the question of his capacity. The Catholic *Wexford Inquirer* opposed him because of his position and religion but it did not mention his physical condition either.

The by-election Arthur fought in Wexford was one of the last before Disraeli's electoral reforms of 1868. You could only vote if you met the minimum property requirement. You had to file a request for voting papers.

The process of proving you had the right to vote was deliberately complicated. Would-be voters had to turn up at the one, and only, polling station and produce their voting papers. Once the sheriff agreed your papers were in order, you could vote. The bureaucracy was designed to exclude, so only 60,000 Irishmen out of a population of just over 5 million could vote. Dublin had 259,000 inhabitants but only 5,264 of them had the ballot. In Wexford there were only about 1,700 voters.

Even those who had the property and the persistence to vote had to do it in public. The fact that there was no secret ballot had predictable consequences. An Irish landlord would see exactly how his tenants voted, for – or against – his man. He would reward the obedient and make the traitors pay.

Arthur spent the day at the polling station, watching the voters come and go. He was nervous something would go wrong but it soon became clear he would win quite easily. His majority was 759 votes when there were less than 2,000 ballots cast. Always wary in public, he was careful not to show how happy he was. When he got back to Borris, Frances congratulated him. Lady Harriett had to admit that her youngest son had surprised her yet again.

One might expect Arthur to be cock-a-hoop. Five years earlier, he had written those depressed lines about his "impossibles". Now he was a Member of Parliament. Everyone in Carlow marvelled at his self-confidence but going to Westminster made him more nervous than anything he had ever done before. Arthur had a sense of history. He wanted to perform well, to make the name of Kavanagh shine again but he was frightened he would be intimidated. Being the master of Borris did not mean very much at Westminster. The House had its celebrities, great men such as Disraeli, Gladstone and the reformer John Bright. Arthur felt dwarfed in every sense.

Throughout I have used Erik Erikson's stages as a useful yardstick. The adult stages of development, as Erikson sees them, are *generavity* versus *stagnation* and, then, *integrity* versus *despair.* But Arthur's career at Westminster doesn't quite fit Erikson's opposites. Arthur always fought for the causes he believed in and, sometimes, he could take unexpected risks. But this "generativity" did not make him feel either secure or happy. His depression didn't melt away. In fact, he would experience a great deal of despair. He tended to see this as the result of his class being under threat but that was not the only reason.

We have seen that Arthur always played down his disabilities and went to great lengths to keep them out of his book on the *Eva.* The Victorian press was no slouch when it came to writing up the careers and personalities of "freaks" and it adored invalid heroes, the cripple who made good. One Irish radical of the time, Michael Davitt, lost his right arm in an industrial accident when he was only 11 years old. The press made much of Davitt's heroism. For the penny dreadfuls, Arthur, limbless in Westminster, was a perfect story, a story Arthur would hate to see in print. I have scoured the contemporary press, the press that revelled in manikins and giants and have found nothing about Arthur going to Westminster. Either he managed to persuade the papers not to write him up or the penny dreadfuls showed unusual restraint.

Arthur took his eldest son Walter with him to the opening of Parliament. The Speaker had agreed his servant could wheel the new M.P. into the chamber. Arthur could not hold the Bible when he swore the Oath of Allegiance so he just had to lay his stump down on it. The moment made a big impression on young Walter who noted, "anyone will realise what it must have been to that shy, sensitive nature under such conditions as his, to face what he had to go through that day. But as his chair is wheeled up to the floor of the House to the table where he has to sign his name, we can hear encouraging cheers coming from all parts of the House."

M.P.s leaned forward to see just how Arthur managed to pick up his pen to sign the register of new members. There were cheers when Arthur seized the pen in his stumps and scribbled his name. He was now, officially, a Member of Parliament.

Arthur had entered Parliament just when the Irish question began to dominate British politics again. We still live with the unfinished business of the political battles of the 1860s and 1870s. Many of the questions Arthur and his contemporaries faced – how to achieve peace, what concessions would persuade the terrorists to back off – are still with us.

I pointed out in Chapter 2 that there have been many studies of the psychological divide between Catholics and Protestants in Ireland since the troubles erupted again in 1969. One robust finding is that children in Ulster become aware very young of which group they belong to. I'm a Prod, you're a Paddy. The world is Them and Us, Black and White, Good and Evil. Arthur sensed that he had to rise above that but he found it a struggle. His "class", as he called it, had to fight or they might lose everything. His wide reading did not reassure him. Arthur was familiar with "revolutionary" arguments. From 1848, when the Communist Manifesto was published, Europe saw much radical rhetoric. Messiah Marx trumpeted the wonders of socialism and communism. The French anarchist Proudhon issued his famous slogan "property is theft". The business of the French Revolution had not been finished, French radicals said. And any revolution threatened not just his money but also his God. Arthur wrote:

> *I can but point to France to prove my position. What happened in the course of her revolution? When Socialism became triumphant was not religion swept away?*

Agitation became one of Arthur's favourite words. He fretted "agitation" would spread. Immoral Irish radicals were fooling good but poor Catholic farmers and "peasants". The Fenians had become even more extreme. Daniel O'Connell "The Liberator" had sometimes depicted himself as a supporter of Queen Victoria but his successors had no time for the Crown. The 1 million Irish in America were to blame. The United States hadn't booted the British out by sticking to Westminster's cosy old rules. The Irish Revolutionary Brotherhood and Clan na Gael wanted to snap the link between Britain and Ireland.

Though Arthur hated the radicals, he often boasted he was something of an Irish nationalist himself. He did not like the English habit of making fun of the "daft" Irish and he did not under-estimate the Fenians. Comerford (1998) points out "Fenian" means advanced man and many of the revolutionaries were intelligent and well educated. Arthur knew that. One of their tactics had a nice irony; they tried to get supporters recruited into British regiments, as that would give them access to weapons.

At first, The War Office did not seem to notice the Fenians' tactics. Then, when the generals realised what the "daft" Irish were doing, the wizards of Whitehall came up with an ingenious solution. Most regiments with large numbers of Fenian sympathisers were transferred to England. This inspired decision only guaranteed more terrorist incidents on the mainland.

Fortunately, the Fenians were as accident prone as British civil servants. Their excellent plans often ended in chaos. The bombing of Chester Castle in February 1867, for example, should have triggered uprisings in Ireland, but the Fenians did not time the bombs right. It all ended in confusion. Then on March 5, there were attacks on police stations in Dublin, Clare, Cork, Limerick and Tipperary but the rebels did not co-ordinate effectively. The rising "failed dismally", according to Devoy in his *Recollections of an Irish Rebel.*

Two Fenian operations, however, did have a big impact on public opinion and on Arthur's views. First, in 1867, the Fenians rescued two men who were being taken to be executed in Manchester. In the process, a Sergeant Brett was killed. A few weeks later, the rescuers were themselves captured, tried and executed. Then, in December came the escape from Clerkenwell Prison. The prison housed the Fenian leader, Richard Burke.

One of Burke's associates, Joseph O'Sullivan borrowed money from a priest to buy some dynamite. Burke was told to stay well away from the prison wall during the exercise period. On the day of the escape, O'Sullivan pushed a pram packed with dynamite down the Clerkenwell Road and parked it against the prison wall. Cool O'Sullivan lit the fuse and sauntered away. A horse was waiting for his leader. The moment the wall blew apart, Burke could run out and gallop to freedom.

But it all went wrong. Burke was not in the exercise yard and the bomb was far too powerful. It destroyed the prison wall but it also killed 12 women and children in a nearby tenement. Press, politicians and public were outraged. It showed, Arthur felt, how depraved the Fenians were. "The English people lost their heads and went into a frenzy of rage against the Irish." Devoy said and added, "The English have a hobby of describing themselves as calm when they have completely lost control of their nerves."

Irish Protestant landlords thought they should make their voice felt. They organised a major rally in Dublin on February 8 1868. Arthur could not be there, but sent a note, which was read out to the crowd. It confirmed his "approbation" of the meeting. A week later he was at Kilkenny Castle with one of the organisers of the rally, the Marchioness of Ormonde. One of the topics they discussed was the poor state of many Irish police stations. The landowners liked to think Ireland's 14,000 police were ever-ready to protect property rights. It was very worrying if the police stations themselves weren't secure.

In a time of such tension, Arthur knew he should say something in Parliament. He could trace his family back to the kings of Leinster. He had been called the landlord of landlords. He knew the Irish situation well. So, no one understood why he did not speak when there was so much to speak about.

1868 – tongue-tied in Parliament

Arthur's fellow Members of Parliament gave him every courtesy. The Speaker allowed William to wheel him into the Chamber. He would place a cushion down so that Arthur could sit and watch proceedings. Arthur never had to struggle to find a place on the benches.

William would wait at the back of the Chamber but in the hubbub of the House, Arthur couldn't always catch his eye. Once in the middle of a debate on lighthouses, William fell asleep and started snoring. Arthur had to ask a fellow Tory to jolt him awake.

Everyone was so kind and it seems that Arthur hated it. He did not want to be pitied. In Borris, he didn't feel awkward. He was among friends. Out East he didn't feel awkward. He was among heathens. But at Westminster, he was among men of his class, the cream of society who ruled the Empire. He couldn't forget his deformities. The Speaker told him he understood it might be an ordeal for Arthur to catch his eye to speak as most members did this by standing up and waving their arms or their hats. He told Arthur he would be prepared to call him at any time, if Arthur let him know in advance he wanted to speak.

The result of everyone being so kind was that Arthur developed stage fright.

In the past, he often got nervous before having to speak. And one result was that he needed to urinate. In Borris that wasn't a problem. In Parliament it was. He hated using the Gentlemen's Cloakroom. The attendant would always smile an encouraging smile, as William wheeled him inside. The chair didn't fit in the toilet. William had to pick him up like a doll.

"Shall I explain to other gentlemen," the attendant asked unctuously, "that . . ."

The attendant's voice was another voice that trailed away in the presence of Arthur, another voice that said and didn't say we don't want to make it hard for the poor bastard. Maybe we should close the gents till the cripple's had his cripple shit. Undignified to have an audience for the sad sod, as his body servant goes into the cubicle, unbuttons his trousers, pulls down his underpants. Do you suppose the cripple's bits are like ours? Can't be really, wouldn't be natural.

William would place Arthur on the water closet and close the door. He would wait outside. Arthur hated hearing footsteps, hated knowing other people knew he was there which they knew as they could see William waiting outside.

Arthur's diary

I would finish my business. I would call "William." I can do many things with my teeth but I won't pull a lavatory chain! William would open the cubicle door and squeeze in. Toilets aren't made for two so he'd have to pick me up with one arm, close the lid of the toilet with the other arm and, then, stand me on the lid. Only then could he attend to me. What did attend to me mean? Clean me up, wipe my arse, flush the toilet, do up my clothes. Walk out to find the attendant smiling a kindly smile!

There would be another ridiculous moment. I always insisted William washed his hands before he picked me up again. He had to perch me on top of the marble basin while he soaped himself.

I sat many days in the Chamber, listening. I tried to picture myself speaking. I tried to imagine getting the Commons to listen, the Commons, the stage of giants – Palmerston, Gladstone, Disraeli, Lord John Russell. I, the half man, 24 inches or some from head to stump, opening my mouth. I shook inside. I needed a cigarette. I wanted to vomit.

Every time I was asked when I would make my maiden speech, I reeled off "soon." I even made up a saying of Art Kavanagh who had angered Richard II. "Speech is silver but silence is golden".

Frances asked me why I had not opened my mouth. Ancient traditions governed maiden speeches, I lied. I didn't like lying to my wife. I felt ashamed at my silence. But I shook and felt sick every time I imagined speaking.

I have always composed homilies to myself in my head, perk you up words of wisdom for the legless and armless. Now they just didn't work. Till Disraeli kicked me up my backside. By the start of 1868 it was clear Dizzy had lost the confidence of the House. He'd have to call a new election. Gladstone might win. I might not be re-elected. I might make history as the only cripple to have sat in the Commons and when historians looked through Hansard they'd find the wonderful cripple man had no arms, no legs and not even a bloody mouth.

I could hear my mother sneer. "You killed your brother Tom and your brother Charley and you couldn't open your mouth."

I finally approached the Speaker. He wrote back saying he was very sorry but I should make my maiden speech on an Irish subject and no Irish debates were planned for the rest of the Parliament. The best I could do, he suggested, was to ask a question "to break your duck", as he put it.

The maiden question

Arthur's first contribution in Parliament was surprisingly slight. In April 1868 he raised the question of lights on the Irish coast. Arthur believed the lack of lighthouses endangered shipping off Wexford and had led to a number of shipwrecks. He wanted to know if there were plans to invest in any new lighthouses. It was a very modest start.

Arthur fought for a number of local causes behind the scenes where he did not get stage fright. He battled to get post office telegraph services established at Borris, he agitated on behalf of a Mrs Ross who had run the poor house and then been denied a pension by the miserable guardians. He raised questions about the safety of ships. He also lobbied constantly for better railway links between Carlow, Wexford and the rest of Ireland. Arthur argued the government had to help finance a centralised Irish railway system, as investors were wary after so many railway companies had succumbed to financial scandals. Nevertheless, Arthur's first term as an M.P. did not achieve much.

At the end of April 1868, Disraeli advised the Queen to dissolve Parliament. But new electoral registers had to be completed first, so Parliament stayed in session until the summer recess. Then, Arthur decided to take a sailing holiday. On 22 August, Arthur set off on the *Eva* with the Marquis of Ormonde and with Captain and

T.E. Holland. They made for Scandinavia, though this time they did not go as far as the Arctic Circle. Arthur returned to Borris eager to fight the new election, which was announced on November 11.

It was clear Ireland would be an important issue again. "The state of Ireland is far more dangerous at this moment than at any former period," said John Stuart Mill in his pamphlet *England and Ireland.* In his campaign, Gladstone thundered that "the state of Ireland after 700 years of our tutelage is . . . an intolerable disgrace."

This time, Arthur stood for County Carlow rather than Wexford. It was natural since Borris was in Carlow, but the Carlow seat had another advantage. Usually the liberals did not put up any candidate. The *Carlow Sentinel* again waxed lyrical about Arthur's qualities.

At his nomination meeting, Arthur sketched out his main positions. Here, among friends, he had no trouble finding the voice he couldn't find at Westminster. "I would watch with a jealous eye private rights." He meant property rights but that did not make him unfair. He pointed to his record as a just landlord, stressing "I have acted precisely the same towards all." At the meeting he raised another issue, which was to stir enormous passion at the time.

Disestablishing the Irish Church

Like the Church of England, the Irish Church was established. Gladstone and other liberals believed that this was not helpful in an essentially Catholic country. It played into the hands of the Fenians. *The Times* agreed and pointed out that the Empire accommodated many different religions. Once the Irish Church was disestablished, the Catholics should repay Queen and Country by giving wholehearted loyalty and spitting on the Fenians. The Indians, Zulus and Hottentots – *The Times* had forgotten the Indian Mutiny, it seems – were all loyal subjects of Victoria, after all.

Arthur told his nomination meeting that he felt strongly about the Church issue. "The object of a State Church is not to make the Church political but to make the State religious," he said. Arthur added "I am not one of those who maintain that her – i.e. Ireland's –

present condition is altogether as could be desired." Nevertheless, the Irish Church should remain established and part of the State.

Irish historians see the 1868 election as the beginning of the process that ended with the establishment of the Irish Free State in 1921. It was a bitter election as it took place against the background of many terrorist incidents and murders.

Arthur won Carlow, unopposed, but he returned to a very different House of Commons in December 1868. Gladstone had won a majority of 112 and he had two main aims – to cut public expenditure and, as he put it, "my mission is to pacify Ireland." Pacifying Ireland meant reforming land tenure, a complex set of issues that would occupy Parliament for the next 14 years. It would show Arthur at his best, and at his worst.

Gladstone was a radical, but not a revolutionary. Proudhon did not tempt him. In a civilised society, property was sacrosanct. Gladstone often looked to the classical world for inspiration. Greek law and Roman law both honoured property rights. The notion of tampering with them was distressing. The new Prime Minister told his new Secretary for Ireland, Charles Fortescue, he was staggered at the possibility of the State interfering with rents and the rights of landlords.

Nevertheless, Gladstone appointed the radical John Bright as Secretary of Trade. Bright helped convince the new Prime Minister to make serious concessions to the Catholic nationalists. There were two options – first, the government could investigate allegations that some Fenian prisoners had been tortured in jail; second, some Fenian prisoners could be freed. But when Gladstone mooted these ideas, he ran into bitter opposition. The Duke of Cambridge complained in the Lords. *The Times* found it outrageous for Irish labourers to collect money for the families of Fenian prisoners. None deserved mercy. Showing any compassion to the Fenian prisoners would be rewarding terrorism. In the end, however, Gladstone did order the release of 41 Fenian prisoners. Arthur, like many others, felt betrayed and disgusted.

The release of the prisoners did not end terrorism. Every week there were political murders. In March 1869, Fenians killed a farmer called Topham in Tipperary. A foul murder, *The Times* said, but Arthur complained some Irish Catholic papers almost gloried in these killings. Cruel landlords deserved a cruel death, they implied. Arthur was also angry with the many Catholic priests who seemed to have lost control of their flocks and refused to condemn the killings. The Pope was no better as he would not disown the Fenians.

Arthur was to have a complex relationship with Gladstone. William Ewart Gladstone was the most intellectual Prime Minister Britain ever had and his approach to Ireland reflected both his moral purpose and his belief in the intellectual approach. Gladstone spent three months reading everything he could find on Ireland – the history of reform attempts like the 1840 Devon Commission, Cromwell's iniquities, the queer customs of Ulster land law, the state of the Irish Church, the Great Famine and the interesting question of how much all the land in Ireland was worth. The Griffiths valuation had put it at £13.6 million. It all led to one simple question. How much would the landlords concede to buy peace?

It is impossible to understand Arthur's political views without some sense of the baroque complexities of Irish land law. In England land was either owned freehold or held on leases of a fixed number of years. In Ireland, there were weird regional complications. In the North, for example, a tenant could not be evicted easily and could sell his so-called "tenant right". But he could only sell that to a buyer the landlord approved and landlord had a say in the price. Landlords nearly always insisted the price should not be too high, almost as if too high a price suggested the tenant had sold too much of the soul of the land.

There were 20,000 Irish landlords but 750 of them owned over half the island. A.N. Wilson in his recent study of the Victorians (2003) damns the vast majority as greedy and callous. The 750 great landlords included grandees like Arthur, Lord Dufferin and Lord Lansdowne; agents usually ran their estates and the agents often bullied – and sometimes brutalised – the tenants. Arthur was unusual in being a very present and hands-on landlord. A few thousand tenants had large holdings but the vast majority of the 600,000 tenants held anything between 3 and 500 acres of land.

Pundits agreed that those who held above 300 acres were fairly well off but small tenants were often as poor as landless labourers. A family needed 30 acres to survive, it was calculated, but half the tenants had 15 acres or less. The population had fallen from 8 million to 5 million because of the Famine but there was still too little land for too many people.

Ancient customs also invited trouble. Five-sixths of the tenants were tenants at will with no leases. Landlords could evict them without much fuss. Greedy landlords faced real temptation. If O'Reilly had improved his acreage, he could be booted out and the spruced up land rented to O'Halloran for £5 more a year. O'Reilly could not prevent it because he had no rights. Intelligently, the Fenians made sure these evictions got as much publicity as possible.

When the House saw the first draft of Gladstone's Land Bill, Arthur objected to many of its clauses. Fenian violence had won concessions, he complained. In the debates, Arthur often spoke as if he were personally offended. He was fair; he did not evict tenants on a whim so why did Gladstone have to offer tenants fixity of tenure? Tales of greedy and unjust landlords were propaganda against Arthur's class. It was black and white again and Arthur minded his class being painted black.

On July 31 1869, Arthur returned to Borris House for the summer recess. He had a great deal to do on the estate but he also wanted to prepare himself for what he saw would be a vital political battle. So, he did not accompany Frances when she left to tour Europe on September 18 1869.

Gladstone was also busy during the summer recess, revising his Land Bill. His new version offered tenants more security of tenure and, for the first time, landlords would have some checks on their actions. They would have to justify increasing rents in front of a tribunal. The whim of the landlord out to squeeze a few more pennies of rent would no longer be enough. The new Bill also offered "compensation for disturbance". If a landlord wanted to evict a tenant for no good reason, he would have to pay for the privilege. The so-called Bright clauses encouraged tenants to buy their holdings though, kow-towing to sacrosanct property, the landlord had to agree. The Board of Works would loan two-thirds of the price.

Gladstone lobbied hard for his Bill and was ruthless towards its opponents. For example, he sniped that one die-hard opponent of

William Gladstone, who liked Arthur.

the Bill, Sir Roundell Palmer "knew no more of land tenure in Ireland than he knew of land tenure on the moon." The lunar Sir Roundell wasn't up to snapping back a good repartee. Arthur was not the butt of such quips because Gladstone knew that the man from Carlow had a good grasp of the complexities of Ireland. And Gladstone hoped that Arthur would be interested in an offer he had made.

Arthur's diary: March 31 1869

I was in the House one evening when a note was pressed into my hand. The Prime Minister wished to see me. Incognito. He was in the habit of taking walks around London at night. Perhaps we could meet at the end of one of these constitutionals.

Gladstone was a practical Christian. Labouchère told me these constitutionals were really prostitutionals. Gladstone talked to women of the streets. "He likes to hear them talk about their activities," Labouchère said. "I don't think he does anything with them. He lectures them on the evils of debauchery. He pays some for the most unusual services. They have to listen to his lectures."

"Maybe he just likes secret adventures and intrigues," I said.

"Of course Gladstone says nothing of this in his writings," Labouchère grinned. "And he never seems to have much interest in the souls of fallen boys, though there are plenty of bum boys in St James."

I did not tell Labouchère that Gladstone had summoned me. I sent Gladstone a note suggesting we meet at the corner of Lupus Street in Pimlico. I was surprised when he suggested two in the morning but he said, he often finished his constitutionals then. He could not sleep easily because his head was so full of ideas.

I leave my house at Tedworth Square with William at 1.30 in the morning. I trust William but I stress he must never speak about this meeting.

"Like the harem is it, master Arthur," William smiles. "I was always sorry I could not be there, attending to you."

"This is a different kind of adventure, William." I send William to wait with the cab driver on the other side of the street.

The bell of St George's, Pimlico, strikes two. I begin to wonder if I have made some ridiculous error. Then, a tap on the door of the cab.

"Mr Kavanagh, I presume." It's Gladstone rich voice.

"Mr Prime Minister!"

He opens the cab door and shifts inside. "Mr Kavanagh," says the Prime Minister, "I hope you don't object to meeting like this."

"I am honoured, though mystified, sir."

"I have great admiration for you, Mr Kavanagh. You have both a sense of justice and an independent mind." He takes out a flask. "Just coffee," he smiles. "Would you like some?"

"I have some Irish whiskey in my flask. I'd like a dram."

Gladstone did not realise I could not drink without his help. Someone always had to get the flask out of my pocket, unstop it, hold it to my lips.

"I need your help, sir," I say

"I am so sorry, Kavanagh." He touches me as he got held of the bottle and held it to my lips. I took a gulp.

"It must be very tiresome for you to have to rely on others to do such things," he said.

"I've been used to it since I was born."

He wasn't used to such intimacy with a stranger. He did not stare at my body but looked me in the eyes. I liked that.

"Unlike many of your Tory colleagues, you don't seem to despise the Irish," he said.

"I'm Irish too ... My ancestors were kings of Leinster. I even studied Gaelic and can read some of the bards."

"Of course," Gladstone nods, "that's why it would be such a help if you could support my new Land Bill."

"Ah," I paused. At least, I now knew why we were meeting. "Do you own land, Prime Minister?"

"Yes."

"Do you feel a connection with it?"

Gladstone has owned his estate for less than 25 years. It belonged to his wife's family, but, of course, I do not say that.

"I feel it especially when I cut down my trees with an axe," he smiles.

"I also cut down trees."

"You won't be offended if I ask how you manage that."

"Place your cane here, sir. Between my stump and my body."

I pressed my stump against the cane. It was well wedged between stump and body and I showed him how I could swish an axe. Gladstone shook his head. "Remarkable, sir. And you get enough chop into the axe."

"I cut down five trees last Saturday."

"Kavanagh, we must work together to save Ireland."

"I want to save Ireland, sir. It's in my blood. I ride out into the fields and the woods and I feel the past. I don't hear voices of the dead crying out to me but I can imagine what it might have been like to till those fields 400 years ago."

"Some of your tenants' families have been there nearly as long."

"But they don't own it or love it or care for it as much."

"Are you sure Kavanagh?"

"Quite sure. I've run my estate for 18 years. I know the good

tenants, the dishonest ones, and the lazy ones. Even the best don't feel about the land as I do."

"I believe in property, Kavanagh, too, but we must," he paused and stared, a dangerous stare, "do something. We have to give the Irish poor hope or even more blood will be shed."

"You want to give them hope by taking away what's mine. I don't see it as mine in a selfish way. I only hold it for my children to hold for their children."

"I respect your feelings, Kavanagh, but I would hope we can work together."

"But how, Prime Minister?"

"If I had your support you could enter the government, you could be one of the Secretary of State's deputies. Fortescue does not know Ireland as well as you do. My reforms are modest," Gladstone smiled. "Imagine what would happen if at the next election, most Irish seats were won by the Fenians. I am under great pressure to introduce secret ballots."

"Pressure from who, sir?"

"Myself. It is not democratic to vote in public. Electors can be intimidated. Your father was I believe guilty of that once."

"That was 35 years ago ... and my father," I fumble the words because I know my father shouldn't have done that.

Gladstone is tactful. "It was 35 years ago, a different age and I'm sure he had his reasons. Everyone in Ireland does. That's why I need your assistance."

"I never saw you, sir, as one who would offer ..." I do not want to use the word bribes.

"Bribes?" he supplies. "I'm only trying to tempt you for the good of Ireland and the Empire."

"I'd be betraying too much, sir, by giving the support you ask."

"Don't be a small minded man, Kavanagh." Gladstone, the towering, the moral mountain.

I want to please him. I want to agree because of his sheer force but he is asking me to betray my history.

"I will keep an open mind, Prime Minister."

"Don't lie to me, Kavanagh. You have no intention of considering my request."

"I don't lie, Prime Minister."

"You could do something useful for your country. You're a thoughtful man. If I were a devil, if I could conjure you up arms and legs, then what would you be so damn proud?"

We stare at each other.

"It's not kind or polite but it's the truth. I'm interested in truth, Kavanagh. I don't think you can face the truth about Ireland. It has to change."

He suddenly sticks his hand out to shake mine and, then, realises I had no hand to shake.

"I apologise," he stumbles, "I had no intention of insulting you that."

"It is very strange that I've never shaken hands with anyone."

"I'm sorry we can't shake hands, Kavanagh. Please think about what I said." Then, he turns away from me and clambers out of the cab.

I am shaking. Gladstone has that effect.

Arthur's first 'big' speech

Arthur never explained what Gladstone said to him on the occasions they met, but it obviously had an impact on him.

Arthur finally made his first speech in the new Parliament on a subject he knew well – the reform of the Poor Law. He tried to balance the rights of the landlords and the needs of the poor. He claimed that if you put all the burden of the poor law on landlords – and people who lived in towns did not have to contribute – it would be grossly unfair. The towns could not survive without the farmers and so the towns should also pay for supporting the rural poor.

The speech was a personal success. Charles Fortescue, the Chief Secretary for Ireland, replied he agreed with much of what Arthur had said even though they were on opposite sides of the House. The Speaker sent Arthur a note, which praised his contribution. The speech also established a consistent theme for Arthur. His class was doing more than its fair share to make Ireland a better place and no one admitted the fact or the sacrifices of the landlords.

Gladstone presented his new proposals to the House on May 31 1869. Remarkably, Arthur did change his mind about Gladstone's Bill. In the debate he announced he would support it. He disagreed with many of the measures and he knew some of his friends would be surprised but Ireland was at a crisis. It was reasonable to make generous offers to the tenants to persuade them of the value of peace. There had been some unjust "ejectments", Arthur admitted for the first time. So there should be a court where tenants could petition against evictions. It was also unfair, he accepted, that tenants who had improved properties should be booted out without any compensation.

Arthur did not find it easy to vote in favour of Gladstone's Bill. When the third reading came, Arthur put down a number of amendments. One insisted that medium to large tenants (whose rents came to more than £100 a year) should not have the special protections the law would offer to small tenants. As the Bill went through the stages in the House, Arthur placed and haggled over amendments. The shy man who did not dare speak in the Chamber had found himself as a House of Commons man.

Gladstone carried the Land Bill in the Commons but the Lords were tougher. The "other place" watered down a number of key provisions and, for the next 12 years, the question of Irish land tenure would constantly re-surface in Parliament. Arthur was never again as radical as he became briefly during these debates in 1870.

On social issues, however, Arthur remained fairly progressive for the next 4 years. One of his most passionate speeches was on the rights of paupers. The English and Scottish authorities could send Irish paupers who arrived on the mainland home. A vagrant called Watson had, been sent back from Liverpool to Belfast in 1871 even though he was suffering from smallpox. His return led to at least 157 deaths in Belfast since no one took the precaution of putting Watson in quarantine. Arthur argued Irish paupers should have exactly the same rights as English, Scottish and Welsh paupers. The State couldn't ferry them where it liked. It was an insult to Irish paupers to treat them differently.

Arthur celebrated five years as an M.P. in 1871 as he hit his 40th birthday. As usual there was a party at Borris and he had something to celebrate. He had established himself as a voice in Irish politics. Curiously, however, Arthur never became a favourite of the Tory leadership. Disraeli did not bother with him but Gladstone, on the other hand, was impressed with him. He said he admired Arthur as a man of "independent mind", even if he "was of the party opposite". Arthur would continue to show his independent mind.

The propaganda war

Throughout the 1870s, the landlords and the so-called "agitators" waged a propaganda war. Mixing satire and paranoia, the *Tipperary Tracts* showed off Protestant prejudices accurately. *The Tracts* claimed to be letters written to a friend in Scotland, which poked endless fun at the Catholics. One tells of an agitator who "was honoured with the largest funeral that ever took place in the parish barring Priest McGuire." Priest McGuire was a "militant Christian, for if we had shot half a dozen landlords he'd never say ill was done." One *Tract* predicted Gladstone intended to buy every acre of land in Ireland and give it to the tenants. Landlords ruined but problem solved! Another *Tract* was more ingenious. Link Ireland with the Holy See. Since the Holy See had lost nearly all its lands in 1870, the Pope needed a few acres and why should his Holiness not have them in Limerick, swapping the Eternal City for the Emerald Isle?

As in modern times, both sides tried to make out they were the real victims. At least Arthur was not revoltingly pious like W. Bence Jones, author of *The Life's Work in Ireland of a Landlord who Tried to Do His Duty.* Asking landlords to give up their rights "would be as treasonable to expect a sheep would co-operate with a butcher who cuts his throat," Bence thundered.

Arthur never made fun of Irish Catholics or sniped that someone's vague allegations were "very Irish" – which many other grandees did. As the 1870s went on, however, his attitudes became more and more dogmatic. He had hoped the support he had given Gladstone would lead to peace and progress. When it didn't, he started to feel more and more that Protestants were being treated unfairly.

"Fenian processions, the noble Earl (Earl of Mayo) now Governor General of India permitted unnoticed or nearly so while Orange processions were stopped by force and their leaders thrown in jail," Arthur complained. He was no Orangeman and he "deprecated" all forms of violence but he wanted even-handed justice.

Arthur saw himself as a fair man and, in many ways, he was. But there was one issue where Arthur's position now seems quite shocking. Gladstone wanted secret ballots in Ireland as well as in England to stop precisely the kind of intimidation Arthur's father had practised when he had "cooped up" his tenants. Irish tenants who didn't vote the landlords' way claimed they would be evicted or their rents would be raised. Gladstone's 1872 Ballot Act was to change all that.

Arthur did not speak in the debate but he voted against the proposals of the Ballot Act. He never tried to justify his position. From his own narrow point of view he was right. It was only after the Ballot Act was passed that a Home Rule Party could put up candidates in Irish elections and the Home Rule Party would change everything forever.

Disraeli wins

Gladstone asked the Queen to dissolve Parliament in January 1874. The Home Rule Party did not stand in Carlow and nor did the Liberals, so Arthur was again returned unopposed. But the election was a disaster for Gladstone. He only managed to hang on to his seat in Greenwich by 403 votes. His arch-enemy, Benjamin Disraeli, became Prime Minister.

For Disraeli, Ireland was not a priority. He already had his eye on the building of the Suez Canal. Nevertheless, from 1874 to 1876 three other important Irish bills were debated in Parliament. They dealt with local elections, gun control and drinking. In every case Arthur had become more of a hardliner.

First, the Liberals proposed a new system of rating, which would change who had the right to vote in local Irish elections. In the whole of Ireland there were fewer voters than in Glasgow, the Liberals argued. Leeds had a population of 259,212 and 52,784 electors. Ireland had only 66,000 electors. Dublin had just 5,284 electors, Belfast 5,525 and Cork just over 2,000.

Arthur was not impressed. People who paid most of the rates should control local administration. Dublin, the one Irish city that used the more democratic English system, was badly run, its streets filthy and waterlogged. For once, Arthur found himself attacked very personally in the House. An M.P. called Dunbar said he was not surprised Arthur wanted the rate system to stay the same, as the proposed changes would quadruple the taxes he had to pay for his estate. Arthur felt offended and Colonel Bruen had to defend him in the House. In the end, Arthur had to deny he had called Dublin a "corrupt" city, and he did get a grudging apology from Dunbar. Arthur then succeeded in winning an amendment that delayed for 6 months the Bill, which meant, in effect, that it disappeared.

When in 1875, the government introduced the Peace Preservation Act, Arthur did not defend the status quo or traditional freedoms. The bill aimed to establish a system of licensing guns. In the second reading debate on March 28th, Arthur had no doubt the State had to control firearms given the level of violence in Ireland. Much as he loved hunting, every hunter would have to have a licence. The Bill also imposed strict controls on who could have a revolver.

But the Peace Preservation Bill also threatened newspapers that published so-called "seditious libels". We tend to romanticise Victorian Britain as a truly free society. Karl Marx worked in London while his friend Engels plotted revolution in Manchester. Britain prided itself on being the home of liberty, but the Bill would jail editors and journalists if they wrote material that was too radical about Ireland. Arthur was in favour of that, as Parliament would prove to be.

Perhaps the most surprising issue where Arthur became less liberal was alcohol. The man who had toured the world in search of good booze and who complained of bad wine in Sweden, spoke in May 1875 "very cordially" in favour of a Bill, which aimed to stop drunkenness in Ireland. Arthur told the House he had originally been opposed to limiting the sale of alcohol, as he didn't like the Irish being put down as a race who could not handle their drink. But the evils of Sunday drinking were all too clear; statistics proved that drunkenness was the second cause of crime in Ireland. First the Fenians, then the Guinness!

The first years of Disraeli's government did see some calm restored to Ireland. There were fewer murders. Some experts believed the Land Act was succeeding; others suggested the very presence of a Home Rule Party at Westminster reduced tension. But the weather also helped; harvests were good and farmers could get credit from the so-called "gombeen men" who toured the counties and offered loans.

The relative calm did not mellow Arthur, however. In terms of Erikson's stages of development, one could argue he was stagnating. He became more stubborn, more insistent on asserting his rights as a landlord. On 29 June 1876, he told the House "I hold my property by immemorial right." New proposals to amend the Land Act made him angry for "it is only necessary for the tenant to be seized with a desire to possess his landlord's property and the chairman of the County is to give him a certificate that he does so." All very ironic, Arthur complained. In the first debates on the 1870 Act, "it was urged on behalf of the Irish tenant that he was so helpless, so ignorant, so imbecilic" that he needed protection, not just from the landlord but also from himself. Now the imbecile was taking over every inch of Ireland.

Every time property rights were threatened, Arthur felt personal outrage. It was an insult, as if no one paid any attention to what a decent chap he had been. He'd played the game, he'd never charged interest to his tenants if they were in arrears, he'd sunk thousands in the estate for the blessed "improvements". He had evicted only six good-for-nothing tenants and always, after giving them every chance to reform. "I have proved my sincerity," Arthur said. But there was no justice for him and his class. Irish revolutionaries wanted flesh, blood, skin and bone.

The summer healed Arthur again. In July 1876, he went sailing in the *Eva* again. He was after ducks in Holland where he bagged a good number. When he returned to Borris, he started to plan an event that meant much to him – the coming of age of his eldest son, Walter. Arthur was not just proud of his eldest son but felt it was important to celebrate what he called "the great tie of clanship," the clanship of the Kavanaghs that went back to the kings of Leinster.

The local gentry, the tenants, everyone in the neighbourhood were invited to the party in Borris House. It was nearly as splendid a do as Arthur's wedding. The band played, the estate was lit by garlands of fairy lights. Walter never had his father's presence and he felt a little intimidated. He made a lacklustre speech. Luckily John Sweetman, one of Arthur's largest tenants, gave a eulogy on the theme of Arthur the perfect landlord, in harmony with the land, in harmony with the tenants. "I defy anyone to show me one single case of harsh treatment on his part towards any of his tenantry," Sweetman told the party.

In return, Arthur made a sentimental speech about the links between landlord and tenant. He recalled when 22 years earlier he had introduced his bride Frances to all his people. He waxed lyrical on the "identity of interest" between landlord and tenant. If he was in the mire, his tenants would be too. If disaster hit his tenants, it affected him too. They were linked, their fates bound together. He told them he felt secure in the people's love. He was utterly sincere and, when they cheered, he believed they were cheering from the heart.

The crops fail again

In 1876, the total value of the Irish potato crop was £12.5 million. But the weather now turned bad again. 1877 and 1878 were too wet and 1879 saw a drought. In 1879, the value of the potato crop fell to £3.35 million. Arthur could see the calm was over.

On January 25 1878, Arthur spoke to yet another set of amendments to the 1870 Land Bill. He was bitter, saying of the Bill "It is like an old enemy. I did not like the Bill when I first saw it and I do not like it now." But eight years earlier, he had voted for it. There was no chance of that now.

In the debate, those who proposed the bill pointed out that there had been 46,414 notices to quit in the previous two years. Arthur accused Nathaniel Buckley, a fellow M.P., of exaggerating the wickedness of landlords because he confused notices to quit for nonpayment of rent with actual evictions. Notices to quit, Arthur pointed out, were often issued to get tenants to pay up.

Then, a new surge of nationalist violence confirmed Arthur in his belief that nothing would satisfy the Fenians. On April 2 1878, the Earl of Leitrim was killed, as he was riding towards an empty cottage from which he had just evicted a widow. "He treated his tenants like dogs," said a local paper, suggesting that justified his death.

By the early summer, farmers faced even more problems as a result of an outbreak of foot and mouth disease. On June 24 1878, Arthur raised a question in the House about whether foot and mouth had been imported from Brussels. He lobbied for a better system of control and, also, for money to train more vets. Untrained farm workers often missed the early symptoms of the disease.

The bad harvest and the foot and mouth outbreak led to a credit squeeze. The City of Glasgow Bank failed. Cash-strapped English companies pressed Irish wholesale merchants who pressed small farmers. The gombeen men were not generous any more but wanted their money back with interest. Arthur seized the moment to point out, both in Parliament and in letters to *The Times*, that often when tenants went bankrupt it was not the landlords who were insisting on getting their money but the banks. But that was a short-sighted point. Bad harvests and economic problems were fertile ground for a new and convincing prophet.

Charles Parnell

In 1877, Charles Parnell replaced Isaac Butt as the leader of the Home Rule Party. Though Butt had created the party, he was never willing to use unorthodox tactics at Westminster. He was too much of a gentleman to be an agitator. Parnell was very different. He came from a Protestant family that had large holdings in the west of Ireland. He said it was the treatment that the Manchester martyrs received in 1867, which had made him a nationalist.

Parnell was a supremely confident man when he entered Parliament in 1875. He had no anxieties about making his maiden speech. Then, almost at once, he started putting pressure on Butt to use more radical methods. Rather like Arthur, Parnell gloried in his family history. His grandfather had been an American naval commander who won a famous engagement in the 1815 war against the British. The President in the White House had received him. Washington was full of the grandsons of the men who had won independence from the British. The lesson was obvious. The best way to drive the English out of Ireland was to harry them, snipe at them and make up new rules which the toffs at Westminster would complain weren't fair. The relative quiet that Gladstone had won with his reforms was about to be shattered.

Arthur hated Charles Parnell for obvious political reasons and for subtler personal ones. He saw Parnell as a traitor to his class. Property rights meant nothing to him. Parnell argued that land, properly speaking, could not be owned by any man. "We went down to Mayo," he once said, "and preached the eternal truth that the land of a country, the air of a country, the water of a country belongs to no man. They belong to the whole human race." As the harvests got worse, Parnell thanked the elements for fighting on his side.

Arthur was cynical about Parnell, saying that "he well knew the lever the prospect of a bad harvest and consequent poverty would give his agitation." But he admitted that Parnell was astute. The agitations of 1879 were "devised with more than ordinary ingenuity." They appealed to the greed of every tenant farmer in Ireland. "Revolution, separation from England and other extreme objects were ... cleverly kept in the background," Arthur sniped. Parnell and his Land League trumpeted tenant right, fixity of tenure and fair rent which "were the ostentatiously adopted mottoes." So the tenants in the North were, for the first time, "made accomplices in a movement the real and ulterior motives of which would, if successful, have wrought their destruction."

Parnell encouraged more attacks on landlords. He did not protest when some were murdered and he even tried to make life easier for offenders as he proposed a bill to ban flogging. Arthur opposed the ban, of course, though he felt he had to justify his hard line. He wrote to a friend "I am as much against flogging as you are but under existing circumstances I did not like to be a party to removing that power from the authorities."

It was against this background of growing unrest that, on March 8 1880, Disraeli announced the dissolution of Parliament. Parnell promised that every Irish seat would be contested. For the first time since 1868 there would be an opposition candidate in Carlow and Arthur would have a real battle. Though the *Carlow Sentinel* again backed Arthur, the *Freeman's Journal* was for his opponent, arguing it was time for a radical change.

Arthur worked hard during the campaign to get pledges of support from his tenants. Nearly all of them, he wrote in his diary, agreed to vote for him. It was desperately important, Arthur said. If Parnell won a large number of Irish seats, the political situation would be changed forever. By the end of the campaign, Arthur was convinced he had done enough to hold on to Carlow, at least. When he went as usual to the polling station in Carlow, he was expecting to scrape a victory. The rest of Ireland might be seduced by Parnell's oratory, but Arthur had been the good master of Borris for 37 years. He had been more generous than any one else of his class. That had to count.

Arthur spent all day at the polling station, hoping that his presence would make those who had promised him their support keep their word. But the secret ballot made the difference. Arthur's tenants no longer had to worry that he would know how they voted.

The result was a resounding defeat for Arthur. He lost by over 700 votes. He worked out that less than 40 of his tenants voted for him. Hundreds had betrayed him. He felt humiliated. He wrote to Frances that he could not bear the fact that so many of those who had promised him their support had lied to him. "That is the poisoned stab," he said.

Arthur put on a brave face, however. He congratulated his opponent and, then, he returned to Borris. Frances tried to console him. So did Walter. It did no good, Arthur sank into a depression. He lay in bed for days, feeling "seedy". He felt he had been betrayed by his people, people he had worked for 28 years. Even hunting and riding did not soothe him in the way they had always done in the past.

Gladstone entered 10 Downing Street for the third time at the age of 71. He was more determined than ever to solve the Irish Question and he was certain the land question was the key to it. The last thing Arthur expected as he drifted through the next weeks was to receive a letter from the new Prime Minister. But Gladstone's plans for Ireland involved Arthur, "the man of independent mind". Arthur would have to deal with a new set of "impossibles", psychological rather than physical ones. He would have to face the possibility of his class giving up more of its power and privileges for the sake of peace with terrorists. Gladstone, at least, was sure Arthur could rise to the challenge.

Chapter 9

The dissident 1880–1882

Gladstone knew about political failure. In 1874 he only just scraped in at Greenwich. When Arthur received Gladstone's letter, he assumed it would be a polite letter expressing sympathy as Arthur had lost his seat. Instead, Arthur discovered Gladstone wanted to appoint him Lord Lieutenant of Carlow County. That was an honour though the post carried only very limited powers. Far more important, Gladstone wanted Arthur to become one of the five men on a committee under the chairmanship of the Earl of Bessborough. The Committee would make new recommendations on how to solve the eternal Irish land question. Arthur accepted at once.

The Bessborough Commission was an impressive body. As well as the Earl of Bessborough, Baron Dowse, the O'Conor Don and William Shaw MP of the Home Rule Party would be Arthur's colleagues. The composition was very Irish but hardly impartial. Four of its members were grandees. Bessborough owned thousands of acres and was known as one of the best landlords in Ireland. Baron Richard Dowse and the O'Conor Don both held substantial lands as did Arthur, of course. It would like having an inquiry today into the oil industry and appointing most of its members from the boards of Shell, BP and Texaco.

The central questions the Commission had to address all stemmed from the 1870 Act. Had it worked? Or were many landlords still unjust? Did they inflict unpredictable rent rises on their tenants? What reforms would calm the situation?

Gladstone told Bessborough he wanted the most thorough study ever of the question and he wanted it fast. By late July, Arthur was in Dublin as the Commission prepared to start work. Sitting in Ely

Street, the Commission heard 700 witnesses. Eighty were landowners and seventy were land agents. The rest were mainly tenant farmers though there was also a smattering of experts like Robert Ferguson QC and Professor Thomas Baldwin who ran a model farm. After they finished in Dublin the Commission behaved a little like a mediaeval assize and pitched its tent all over Ireland, taking over the best local hotel for its sessions. The 1300 pages of evidence the Commission produced gave an immensely detailed picture of Irish rural life – its contents, discontents and controversies.

The Commission also studied land tenure in other countries. John Sweetman argued that in France and Belgium peasants often had tiny holdings of land, but still managed to make a living from them. Lord Dufferin reported on experiments in Tzarist Russia. There was evidence about how landlords in Minnesota provided poor farmers with tools and other equipment. One issue was whether to give landless peasants some land in the hope that would, in modern jargon, make them stakeholders.

There is a scholarly monograph to be written on the Commission's work but, as this is a biography, I concentrate on Arthur's role. In the last chapter I suggested Arthur had been influenced by many of the writings surrounding the Paris Commune. It's easy to poke fun at Arthur who at times seems to be arguing one must not discriminate against a persecuted aristocracy, but he sincerely felt that was what Gladstone wanted to do. Sacrifice the landlords for the Fenians. With memories of the terror in Carlow in 1840, that was "an impossible" for him. And yet he knew something had to be done. It's this tension that made the next 2 years difficult for him.

The Commission started formal hearings on September 1 1880. Arthur's questions to the first witness, Mr E. Moleyns QC, reflected his concerns. Arthur fretted about the rights of landlords. Discussing the number of "ejectments" as evictions were called then, Arthur asked; "Can there be ejectments not at the suit of the landlord?" De Moleyns agreed that, often other creditors, including the banks and their gombeen men, started eviction proceedings when tenants got in arrears with their debts.

Arthur then asked a land agent, Henry Ormsby, if it was not true that there had also been "a great increase in receivers" who had been appointed by the courts to take over bankrupt estates. Yes, said Ormsby. If so, Arthur pounced, that showed "a greater number of landlords have got into difficulty than formerly." Why if the landlords were monsters exploiting the poor?

The Commission had to examine the possibility of forcing landlords to sell land to tenants. Arthur was, of course, hostile."You don't approve as a universal scheme that the land of Ireland is to be handed over from the owners to the occupier on the spot," he asked Ormsby.

Ormsby certainly did not approve.

Another area of controversy concerned improvements to the land, who should pay for them and benefit from them? John La Touche owned three estates and Arthur asked him to imagine a situation. He rents out a farm. To encourage the farmer to improve the property, La Touche offers a low rent. The lease comes to an end. Would La Touche then give the farmer a new lease again at a low rent in recognition of these improvements?

That would be giving the farmer too much help, La Touche insisted. One period of low rent was quite enough. But peasant proprietorship would have benefits "if you could create such a class" because "it would enlist them on the side of law and order." But La Touche also expressed a familiar English worry. Give the feckless Irish any stake in the land and they would booze and gamble it away. Arthur also feared that if tenants could subdivide land, they would eventually subdivide so much, people would be left only with "potato gardens".

But some "Establishment" witnesses disputed this unflattering view of the Irish. On September 3, the Reverend Patterson from Kildare told Arthur, "I believe there is no more frugal or industrious race under Heaven if they have sufficient motive given them but no man on earth will work without a motive."

The Reverend was also a farmer and he knew that land law often led to sin. Tenants should be saved from land hunger and from themselves, he argued, because lust for land "urges men to great intrigue. They go into the landlords' office and offer him impossible things in order to get the land over each others heads." Patterson would not join in the "outcry against landlords. But they must see the despicable phases of human nature" as man fought man for land. Many tenants offered rents they could never manage just to have that extra acre.

Both sides were trying to persuade the Commission that they were victims, of course – the tenants victims of brutal landlords, and the landlords victims of the Fenians. One problem Arthur faced was that he could see many of the agents were arrogant as he had once felt Doyne was.

On September 9, The Commission heard Alexander Kirkpatrick, agent to Lord Portalington. "He has no equal in all of Ireland," Kirkpatrick boasted of his employer. When Arthur came to examine Kirkpatrick, he asked, "Is it not a fact that many of those evictions so-called on the part of landlords might have taken place at the suit of other creditors."

Kirkpatrick readily agreed. The landlords were not the only guilty ones. But Arthur wanted to show more. Landlords were a power for good. He believed in the value of contact between landlord and tenant, and he was waiting for a witness to let him to expand on his views. Finally he got his wish, the ideal witness. James O'Connell of Cork had taken over the family farm after his father died. The agent increased the rent. Unusually, O'Connell ran another business and so he felt strong enough to argue. The land had not been revalued so what justified the rise in rent? The agent was having none of that cheek. He then insisted O'Connell let a large consignment of timber be transported across his farm. No, said O'Connell. There was a perfectly good alternative route. His crops might be damaged if timber were dragged across his land.

The agent started to threaten O'Connell with eviction. The fact that O'Connell could afford the fare to London now became crucial. O'Connell set off for Eaton Square and asked to see his landlord, the grand Lord Egremont. His Lordship turned out to be the very model of Arthur's perfect landlord. His Lordship understood. The agent was being too hard. O'Connell had a point. Noblesse doesn't just oblige but understands. There would be no rent rise, no hauling of timber across the fields. The tenant was blessed with a wise and gentle landlord. Harmony between the classes could exist.

Arthur pounced on the moral of the tale. "You think it was going to the landlord that saved him," he asked.

Indeed, it was, O'Connell agreed.

A land auctioneer, William Doherty, then complained of absentee landlords. In his native Innishowen Doherty said the absentee landlords "extract £2 an acre for very inferior land." Too many landlords spent no time with their tenants. When landlords deigned to visit their estates, "they are surrounded by guards of agents and sub agents." The agents intimidated tenants and prevented the landlord talking to any of them. Which would lead to more harmony?

Arthur also felt there was a risk Gladstone would force landlords to sell their estates. On September 6, he had a spat with a 440-acre tenant, John Derham, asking him; "Would you force the landlord to sell his estate whether he liked it or no?"

Derham didn't give the clear 'yes' or 'no' Arthur expected. He argued instead there were three sorts of landlords. The absentee landlord, the prodigal who had frittered away his inheritance and now desperately needed to squeeze every last penny out of the land, and large companies. Derham would force companies like the Law Life Society to sell out to their tenants.

On this point, Arthur had an interesting exchange with Edward O'Brien. O'Brien had been a tenant farmer for 18 years and argued tenants should have the right to buy the land they rented and that the Board of Works should provide finance as it had done under the Bright clauses. The law should offer the landlords protection against injustice, O'Brien said. "and I mean pecuniary injustice for you cannot put a value on a landlord's feeling."

"I am afraid it is too late for that now," Arthur replied, speaking for his class, which had suffered so much.

On September 13, the Commission adjourned its hearings in Dublin. In 2 weeks, they had listened to over 100 witnesses – an impressive work rate. A week later, the Commission reconvened at the Imperial Hotel in Belfast to find out just how well the tenant right system worked in the North. Was this part of the solution?

There was a problem, however. The Commission did not have the documents setting out the precise terms of the 1614 Plantation of Ulster until they got to the North. By the time the documents were found, the evidence from witnesses was making it clear the situation in the North was far from perfect. There had been the famous "boycott" – the word comes from the incident when a

Captain Boycott's land was "boycotted" by local priests and nationalists. The Captain persuaded his fellow landlords to hit back. They drafted in labour from the Orange Lodges of Belfast to harvest the crops and show the Fenians who was boss.

Some Ulster witnesses had a nice irony. The Camlough Tenant Right Association, for example, put up a spokesman, Patrick O'Callaghan from Lisrevagh played to the audience.

Arthur: Mr Richardson is one of the best landlords in Ireland?
O'Callaghan: Yes.
Arthur: Does he give any allowance for improvements?
O'Callaghan: Not a penny.
Arthur: Does he make any improvements himself?
O'Callaghan: No, he does not assist in any way.
Arthur: Why is Mr Richardson one of the best landlords in Ireland then?
O'Callaghan: He does not raise rents like many landlords who raise rents before the end of the lease and if the lives in the lease are gone to America the tenant has to prove they are still alive.

Richardson was good, in other words, because most landlords were so bad.

Pharoah's land agent

Arthur enjoyed some of the exchanges with witnesses, even if they were his ideological opponents. Joseph Beatty of Keonan had delved in Genesis and based his arguments on the fact that Joseph was the land agent for Pharaoh. After various warnings (usually, of course, in the form of plagues) from Jehovah it was decreed that the fair rent for Pharaoh to get was one-fifth of the revenue from a piece of land.

Beatty had calculated his 68 acres had earned £408 last year, which meant that he should be paying £1 and 4 old shillings; he was, in fact, paying £1.10s an acre

"Who is your Pharoah," Arthur asked in the spirit of these exchanges.

"Lord Downshire," Beatty replied.

When the Commission went to Londonderry on September 27, they sat at Jury's Commercial Hotel where they heard Joseph Alexander. Though just an ordinary tenant farmer, he had studied 60 tenant proprietors and his findings contradicted orthodoxy. Even though many of these 60 held less than the breakeven 30 acres, only three holdings were in poor condition. The rest were thriving and Alexander did not know of a case of foolish subdivision.

In Londonderry, the Commission also heard its first anonymous witness who complained bitterly of the Duke of Abercorn. The Duke was a bully who raised rents whenever he felt like it. The anonymous witness got backing from an unlikely source. On September 30, Hugh McKinley told the Commission he had been a land agent for 27 years "so you will not think my evidence biased against the landlord when I tell you I have known families having to pay the rack rent and then live off charity for 3 months." On many estates subdivision worked in the landlords' favour, McKinley said, as tenants had to pay a penalty to the estate if they subdivided.

Four members of the Commission were coming to see that, even if many landlords were decent, many were greedy and ruthless. Old complaints were not frivolous or the result of mouthing Parnell's line. But Arthur was not yet willing to concede the landlords were "evil," as he showed when he examined Martin Raphael.

Martin Raphael had been a receiver for the Court of Chancery in Connemara. He alleged there had been many evictions. Arthur pressed him to name names, Raphael fingered the Law Life Society as one of the worst offenders but Arthur wanted details before he believed that.

Arthur: Can you state positively it occurred?
Raphael: I can state positively it occurred.
Arthur: In many cases?
Raphael: In many cases.
Arthur: On the Law Life Society estate?
Raphael: Yes.

Arthur: Was that since Mr Berridge became the agent?
Raphael: No before.
Arthur: Was it done by Mr Robinson when he was the agent?
Raphael: Of course it was done by Robinson but chiefly by Mr Robertson, his predecessor.
Arthur: How long since these cases occurred?
Raphael: I cannot tell how long.
Arthur: My questions were as to evictions since the Land Act.
Raphael: They were more numerous before.
Arthur: Then the Land Act has had some effect in stopping them?

Arthur wanted to establish things had changed, that many of the scandals Raphael referred to were ancient, 10, even 15 years old. They belonged to the Ireland before the Land Act. But Raphael insisted the abuses were still going on.

The woes of the west

As the Commission went to the west of Ireland, they found mounting evidence of the greed and bad behaviour of the landlords. One small tenant, Michael Heffernan, pointed out he paid £27 and 10 shillings and did not get a penny towards improvements. Edward Toole told Arthur "we never got a farthing of help from the landlord", though he had upped the rent from £9 to £13.

There were some dramatic confrontations. A Colonel Daly presented himself as a model landlord but one of his tenants complained the model Colonel charged too high rents. Arthur had to umpire an argument between Sir William Verene and one of his tenants who alleged he had been forced to sign a document, which required him to lease a useless bog if he wanted any decent land.

The most lurid stories of the abominable landlord came from James Brady of Glencolen. He complained of a landlord called McKeown who often hit tenants when he had too much whiskey. McKeown was always broke and, sometimes, stole his tenants' cattle. He took them back to his own "pen" and the tenants had to ransom their own cows for 2/6. One old woman, alleged Brady, had had to give McKeown a hen "to get a cow he had put in his pen liberated." McKeown got his come-uppance. He set fire to a barn and, since he was too drunk to get out, he burned to death. Hardly Arthur's kind of landlord.

The Commission then returned to Dublin to hear one of the great authorities on Irish agriculture, Professor Thomas Baldwin. The Professor ran a model farm near Dublin. On November 16 1880, he lectured them for a whole day. Rents were too high, the further West one went the worse the landlords behaved and in Minnesota it all worked better because, of course, most of the farmers were German.

The next day, one of the grandees, Lord Dufferin, argued that radical reform was essential. He was the Jonah whose ears Arthur had pierced long ago."I believe we shall never have a contented or tranquil Ireland until the great proportion of the lands of Ireland have passed into the hands of the people of this country," he said. Dufferin had no intention of handing his lands over without compensation but he pointed out the Exchequer spent £3 million a year on "Irish projects". Dufferin calculated it would be possible to raise £100 million if one were willing to pay £3 million in interest a year. The value of all the land in Ireland had been set some years earlier at £13.6 million by the Griffiths valuation in the 1850s. It was worth far more now, Dufferin agreed, but it would still take far less than £100 million for the state to buy out all the Irish landlords.

Dufferin asked the Commission to look at what was happening in Russia. There, landlords had been forced to yield some land and the government then leased parcels of land directly to tenants. Each town was responsible for interest repayments back to Moscow. If Igor of Minsk did not pay his rent on time, his neighbours would badger him because they would have to pay extra to make up for his irresponsible behaviour.

On November 30, the Commission held its final hearing but soon there was a problem. Landlords and agents who had been accused of bullying, increasing rents and unjust evictions demanded the right of reply. Arthur and Bessborough agreed to hold additional sessions between the 3rd and 10th of January 1881 at Ely Place. There was also a mass of written evidence. Bruen presented a complex set of calculations of the value of the land on behalf of landlords.

By the middle of January the Commission had listened to all the objections and the five men settled to writing the report. We have seen that some landlords like Dufferin were willing to see radical changes. So, Arthur fretted, were Bessborough and Dowse. As the Committee tried to hammer out its report, Arthur felt these two men were willing to make too many concessions to the Land League position. He found himself increasingly isolated. He was just not able to agree to such radical change.

And then, Anthony, his second son fell gravely ill on board the ship where he was serving. Arthur was always a loving father. He was distraught and it brought back memories of Tom's death at sea forty years earlier.

The final report

It seems likely that this personal tragedy made Arthur even more inflexible.

There were many battles between the Commissioners. In the end, the report was only approved in full by two of the five commissioners, Bessborough and Dowse. The O'Conor Don argued more for peasant proprietorship, as did Shaw, who did represent the Home Rule party. They nevertheless signed the main report though both men also published appendices detailing their views.

The Bessborough report recommended the so-called Three Fs – free sale, fixity of tenure and fair rents. It concluded the Land Act had failed to give the Irish people security and "the extent and mischief of this feeling of insecurity" badly affected the country. Many estates were decently managed, but "a great part of landlords are doing everything they can to put down the Land Act of 1870. We regard the present condition of affairs as a symptom of a deep seated disorder of the body politic."

The main recommendations were radical. First, tenants should be given fixity of tenure. Second, they should have the right to go to arbitration to fix fair rents. Third, tenants should have the right to sell what remained of their lease. All these "concessions" lessened landlords' rights but the Commission thought the greatest loss would be a "sentimental one". Many landlords had "powerful feelings" about the land they owned and would resent interference but it was "a concession to justice". A once and only concession, the Earl of Bessborough warned, because these recommendations shouldn't be seen as a "first instalment", a down payment on the way to separating Ireland from England.

Bessborough put Arthur under intense pressure but he refused to sign the main report. He insisted on issuing his own minority report, which was printed with the formal report and also presented to Parliament in March 1881.

Arthur did not accept that the Land Act had failed, as it had "materially checked" the number of evictions. Many complaints of raising rent "have been simply childish", he added. His report is ambivalent throughout. On the one hand, many allegations against the landlords had not been proved; on the other hand, "sufficient instances have been shown to have occurred of what would appear to be the unjust exercise of these powers." The Land Act had not stopped "the power to raise rents in unscrupulous hands." So, Arthur accepted a system of arbitration because unjust landlords left no alternative.

Arthur pointed out the "in the shibboleth of agitation, Fixity of Tenure and Free sale are coupled together as if they were one term but I cannot regard them in that light." Nearly everyone, whatever their class, wanted to see some form of fixity of tenure but Arthur was not prepared to give tenants that absolutely.

Free sale, Arthur argued, caused far more controversy – even among tenant farmers. It would increase differences between the rich and the poor because only those tenants who had capital could buy land and that would "preclude a very considerable proportion of the population whose only capital is their labour." Landlords could be encouraged but must not be forced to sell. He made it personal. He added he had "no disinclination whatever to extend this right (free sale) on my own property even though I have spent very large sums on improvements."

This was giving enough to the agitators. Justice didn't demand any more. Though he had tried to eliminate "all revolutionary proposals," Arthur's own proposals did curtail the rights of landlords. The State should therefore agree to buy at a fair price the estates of those landlords who did not want to operate in these new conditions.

At the end of his one-man report Arthur turned to terrorism. He wanted protection for "the assertion of just rights" and summary punishment of those who took or re-took lands by terror. Landlords as well as tenants were suffering from the present "lawless state of affairs". The proceedings of the Land League favoured "the most extreme, communistic and revolutionary laws which no legislature can fulfil or satisfy." In the west of Ireland people were so poor that giving them rights didn't mean anything. Most labourers were called farmers but had no farms. Arthur floated one other idea – encourage emigration to Western Canada.

Gladstone introduced the new Land Bill in April 1881. The political truth was stark. Arthur had lost, Bessborough had won. There was a rearguard action in the Lords. Arthur's one-man report was quoted by Lord Hagan who said it highlighted all the problems with Gladstone's new Bill. Arthur missed being able to take part in these debates. Luckily *The Times* gave him a great deal of space to explain his views.

On April 22 1881, Arthur had a three-column letter in *The Times.* He argued, "the fact that there was grievance gave the hope that the grievance might be fair." On the Commission, he had been cheered because "the evidence of majority of tenant farmers which was fair and honest, repudiating communism and such wild views gave strength to that hope." He would accept a Court of Settlements for rents so landlords could not demand unjust amounts. "I would increase the penalty for capricious evictions," he said even though Irish tenants were "most litigious".

"I am not going to raise a dirge about the disestablishment of my class. If it is for the welfare of the commonwealth that we should go, so be it . . ." But he did not find it easy to let go. He accused that "this part (of the Bill) is drawn in a spirit of bitter hostility to the landlord class. If there are ways to punish the landlord, the Court is directed to adopt the one that will hurt him most."

Gladstone's new proposals did not mean an end to violence, which did not surprise Arthur. He believed the Land League "has been efficiently although secretly, kept up and the spirit which fed it has always been present." Supporters of the Land League therefore had a "matured organisation upon which to begin work." On July 24 there was a shooting in Phoenix Park.

Many advocates of tenant right, Arthur claimed, see "it is a cure for all evils." He added that the Prime Minister and the Attorney General for Ireland claimed that the Bill "takes nothing landlords from which they ought to be compensated." Not for Arthur. For him, the Bill was a "blot on the statute book."

The death of his second son, losing the argument on the Commission all left Arthur depressed. But Arthur was never a quitter. Despite all the reverses, he kept on writing letters to *The Times* outlining the many reasons why he felt Ireland would not achieve peace if the landlords were treated unfairly. And though he was now out of Parliament, he could still fight for what he believed in.

Chapter 10

"The best and ablest Irishman alive"

At the age of 52, Kavanagh was still a sprightly man. He had not given up on the hope of persuading the government to adopt some of his ideas. When I planned this book I was tempted to assume that at one point Kavanagh went to visit the Elephant Man who was then living in the London Hospital from 1884. Both the Elephant Man and Arthur were famous. But though I have looked and hoped to find, there is no suggestion in Arthur's journals that he ever made the trip from his house at Tedworth Square to the London Hospital in Whitechapel where Frederick Treves had arranged accommodation for John Merrick.

Nevertheless, there are some interesting parallels between the two men. Merrick described how he became increasingly depressed in his youth as he realised the full extent of his deformity and how that would affect him. Treves had noted that Merrick's moods changed very dramatically.

Merrick had to struggle with practical issues that never bothered Arthur, mainly that of how to survive financially. He had had to allow himself to be exhibited as the Elephant Man. But, money aside, both men had to cope with many of the same problems – their bodies made them utterly different to other men. Merrick was much more open about his depressions and he did not express himself in euphemisms, as Arthur did when he said he often felt "seedy".

But in Arthur's case, the political situation also gave him no joy. Before he had written his minority report, he was already sensing he faced a battle. At the start of 1882 Arthur was meant to attend a meeting of "the great aggregate of the landlords of Ireland" but he was unwell. He sent a message of support as it now seemed to him vital that landlords should defend their interests. Ten months later, he wrote to *The Times* (October 12th) and the letter has a whiff of paranoia. It claimed that the government had sent out "secret instructions" concerning the judicial reviews of rent – these secret instructions that would ensure that judges had been told to decide cases in such a way that the landlords would get less rent. The Secretary of State for Ireland, Fortescue, replied immediately to him, thundering, "I cannot allow a gentleman of such high authority of Irish matters and one for whom I have so much personal regard" to be misinformed and to put out such misinformation.

Kavanagh replied that Fortescue would therefore hardly mind if Kavanagh sent his letters to the papers.

Arthur felt that the landlords needed an organisation to counter the Land League. He decided to set up an organisation called The Land Corporation of Ireland which aimed to protect the rights of landlords. He raised £274,000 to help it start.

The 1885 election

Ironically given his opposition to the secret ballot, as the 1885 election neared, Arthur felt impelled to say there was no secret ballot in Ireland. He blamed the thuggery of Parnell and his supporters for that because they used such intimidating tactics. John Morley, the new Secretary for Ireland, asked "Why is it that the Irish are in many respects poorer, more ignorant, more backward." And Morley answered it in a way that infuriated Arthur. "It is because of the landlords who have rackrented them, ... sunk them into poverty, plundered their improvements, have confiscated the fruits of their labour."

Arthur again wrote to *The Times* and warned that the Land League was intimidating the peasants. "An order has gone out" to stop tenants behaving sensibly.

On November 12, 1885 Kavanagh had another letter published in *The Times.* He warned that the majority of readers fail to grasp the real position of affairs in the country. Arthur agreed that Parnell's popularity should be tested but "a system of terrorism and intimidation is spread over the land which has rendered freedom of action impossible and turned the meaning of the words independent electors into a farce."

It took courage for any one to vote against Parnell in some areas. "One important fact is to be borne in mind," Arthur added. The irony was that although the secret ballot had been introduced back in 1874, "the lower classes in Ireland do not believe in the secrecy of the ballot." It was a strange irony, he admitted.

An excellent sense of the work of the Land Corporation and of Arthur's mood comes from an account by an anonymous writer, who toured Ireland and reported on his meetings with landlords, tenants, lawyers and other interested parties. This appeared in *Blackwood's Magazine*.

On March 2 1886, after visiting Cork the author went to Borris which he described as "lovely, picturesque, richly-wooded land it is. Rural scenery quite unlike anything I have hitherto seen in Ireland. At Bagnalstown, a very pretty place, with a spire which takes the eye, our host joined us, and came on with us to this still more attractive spot. Borris has been the seat of his family for many centuries." Many Kavanaghs, the author noted, "lie buried in the ruins of St Mullen's Abbey, on the Barrow, in this county. But none of them, I opine, ever did such credit to the name as its present representative, Arthur MacMorrough Kavanagh."

The author had corresponded with Kavanagh and knew in detail his "striking views on the condition of Irish affairs – views since abundantly vindicated." Meeting Arthur was remarkable, "and like most people who have paid any attention to the recent history of Ireland, I knew how wonderful an illustration his whole career has been of what philosophers call the superiority of man to his accidents, and plain people call the power of the will. But I knew this only imperfectly. His servant brought him up to the carriage and placed him in it. This it was impossible not to see. But I had not talked with him for five minutes before it quite passed out of my mind. Never was there such a justification of the paradoxical title which Wilkinson gave to his once famous book, *The Human Body, and its Connexion with Man* – never such a living refutation of the theory that it is the thumb which differentiates man from the lower animals."

The author added:

> *Twenty times this evening I have been reminded of the retort I heard made the other day at Cork by a lawyer, who knows Mr Kavanagh well, to a priest of "Nationalist" proclivities, who knows him not at all. Some allusion having been made to Borris, the lawyer said to me, "You will see at Borris the best and ablest Irishman alive." On this the priest testily and tartly broke in, "Do you mean the man without hands or feet?"*

It was not just Arthur who impressed the author. He was delighted by Borris but Frances insisted the estate was not looking its best.

"You should see this view in June," said Mrs Kavanagh, "we are all brown and bare now."

Brown and bare, like most other terms, are relative, the author noted. The loveliness of the estate pleased him. The next morning, the author strolled on the lawn and talked to Arthur about the Land Corporation. Arthur explained that "when a landlord has been driven into evicting his tenants, the next step, in the 'war against landlordism,' is to prevent other tenants from taking the vacated lands and cultivating them. This is accomplished by 'boycotting' any man who does this as a 'land-grabber'." He added "The ultimate sanction of the 'boycott' being 'murder,' derelict farms increased under this system very rapidly; and the Eleventh Commandment of the League, 'Thou shalt not pay the rent which thy neighbour hath refused to pay,' was in a fair way to dethrone the Ten Commandments of Sinai throughout Ireland."

Arthur then told a story of how in 1885, a parish priest, the Rev. Mr Cantwell, described it as a "cardinal virtue" that "no one should take a farm from which another had been evicted," and called upon the people who heard him to "pass any such man by unnoticed, and treat him as an enemy in their midst." In his native America, the author added, "public opinion and the law, if not the authorities of his church would make short work of any priest who talked in this fashion."

But Ireland was different. It was because the government had made, and was making too many concessions to the Land League, Arthur had founded the Land Corporation. If landlords were driven from any properties, the Corporation would step in to manage them.

The Land League slandered, no surprise, those who worked for the Corporation. Arthur spoke of a certain Father Keller who described them as a set of desperadoes or "enfants perdus". But Arthur insisted they were really "a body of resolute and capable working men farmers. Many, but by no means all of them, are Protestants and Ulstermen."

The author was struck by the fact that farmers who were in the Land Corporation did not usually get driven off from the holdings confided to them. "A great part of the Luggacurren property of Lord Lansdowne is now worked by the Corporation; and Mr Kavanagh was kind enough to let me see the accounts, which indicate a good business result for the current year on that property. This is all very interesting. But what a picture it presents of social demoralisation! And what is to be the end of it all?"

Committed as he was to the cause of the Corporation, Arthur did not neglect his duties as a host. In the afternoon, he took the author for "a delightful walk through the woods, Mr Kavanagh going with us on horseback. Every hill and clump of trees on this large domain he knows, and he led us like a master of woodcraft through all manner of leafy byways to the finest points of view. The Barrow flows past Borris, making pictures at every turn, and the banks on both sides are densely and beautifully wooded. We came in one place upon a sawmill at work in the forest, and Mr Kavanagh showed us with pride the piles of excellent timber which he turns out here. But he took a greater pride in a group, sacred from the axe, of really magnificent Scotch firs, such as I had certainly not expected to find in Ireland."

Arthur was still fascinated by history and his family's history. He showed off his library. "There are many curious old books and papers here, and a student of early Irish history might find matter to keep him well employed for a long time in this region." I suspect that some of the documents I saw over 100 years later were the very same ones.

The author of the *Blackwood*'s article also gave a good feel for what Borris was like in the mid-1880s. "This is a staunch Protestant house, and Mr Kavanagh himself reads a Protestant service every morning. But there is little or nothing apparently in this part of Ireland of the bitter feeling about and against the Catholics which exists in the North. A very lively and pleasant Catholic gentleman came in to-day informally and joined the house party at luncheon. We all walked out over the property afterwards, visiting quite a different region from that which we saw yesterday – different but equally beautiful and striking, and this Catholic gentleman cited several cases which had fallen within his own knowledge of priests who begin to feel their moral control of the people slipping away from them through the operation of the "Plan of Campaign." I told him what I had heard in regard to one such priest from my ecclesiastical friend in Cork. "It does not surprise me at all," he said, "and, indeed, I not very long ago read precisely such another letter from a priest in a somewhat similar position. I read it with pain and shame as a Catholic," he continued, "for it was simply a complete admission that the priest, although entirely convinced that his parishioners were making most unfair demands upon their landlord to whom the letter was addressed, felt himself entirely powerless to bring them to a sense of their misconduct."

Arthur gave a number of examples of how landlords had been disadvantaged. He told at some length the story of the troubles on the O'Grady Estate. The O'Grady of Kilballyowen was the direct representative, not of any Norman invader, but of an ancient Irish race. "If there be such a thing – past, present, or future – as an 'Irish nation,' the place of the O'Gradys in that nation ought to be assumed." Arthur said. Since the 1840s land had been let to the tenants at rents which had to be fair, since they had never been raised.

Trouble only started in 1886. Six tenants refused to pay and were evicted. "All of these lived in good comfortable houses, and were prosperous dairy-farmers." Then, in October 1886, during the candidacy of the Land Reformer, Mr George, Mr Dillon, M.P., propounded the "Plan of Campaign" at Portumna in Galway. The March rents were due; O'Grady's agent in Limerick, Mr Shine, was told to continue the abatements of 15 per cent, on the judicial rents, and of 25 per cent, on all other rents, which had been cheerfully accepted in 1885. But a priest at Kilballyowen, Father Ryan, urged the tenants to demand a reduction of 40 per cent. This was refused;

then, they asked for 30 per cent on the judicial rents, and 40 per cent on the others. This was also refused so the inflammatory Father Ryan had his way.

As they got no rents. O'Grady's issued writs against several of the tenants.

Finally in the spring of 1887, O'Grady's tenants offered to accept a general abatement of 17½ per cent. But they wanted the landlord to pay all the costs. This made O'Grady furious and he issued a circular arguing that "I am a resident landlord; my ancestors have dwelt amongst you for over 400 years; every tenant is personally known to me, and the most friendly relations have always existed between us."

But the tenants still refused to pay the rents.

O'Grady subsequently took proceedings against six other tenants, who refused to pay rent, and removed their cattle off the land to avoid payment, and having got judgment against them, the Sheriff sold four of their farms. The landlord also got judgments for possession against two other tenants for non-payment of rent.

Trying to be emollient, O'Grady offered to allow the 17½ per cent all round on payment of one year's rent and costs, and to give time for payment of the costs. His offer was refused.

"I never commenced these proceedings in a vindictive spirit, or with any desire to punish any of you for your ungracious conduct." O'Grady said, "but simply to protect my property from unjust and unreasonable demands". He added he would now accept a reduction of 20 per cent all round, on payment of a year's rent and costs. But there was one point on which he would not budge. The tenants had put him to all this trouble and they had to pay, in full, the costs of the various actions that they had caused.

All the evictions had since been carried out, Arthur said and the Land Corporation men are at work upon the estate!

The author asked rhetorically "Whom has all this advantaged? The tenants? – Certainly not. The O'Grady? – Certainly not. The peace and order of Ireland? – Certainly not. But it has given the National League another appeal to the intelligent 'sympathies' of England and America. It has strengthened the revolutionary element in Irish society. It has 'driven another nail into the coffin' of Irish landlordism and of the private ownership of land throughout Great Britain."

The author got Arthur's very direct views on being a landlord.

"I have the agencies of several properties," Arthur told him, "and in some of the best parts of Ireland. I have had little or no trouble on any of them, for I have one uniform method. I treat every tenant as if he were the only man I had to deal with, study his personal ways and character, humour him, and get him on my side against himself. You can always do this with an Irishman if you will take the trouble to do it. Within the past years I have had tenants come and tell me they were in fear the Plan of Campaign would be brought upon them, just as if it were a kind of potato disease, and beg me to agree to take the rent from them in that case, and just not discover on them that they had paid it before it was due!"

The author continues: "As a public man, familiar for years with the method and ways of British Parliaments, Mr Kavanagh seems to regard the possible future legislation of Westminster with more anxiety and alarm than the past or present agitations in Ireland. The business of banishing political economy to Jupiter and Saturn, however delightful it may be to the people who make laws, is a dangerous one to the people for whom the laws are made. While he has very positive opinions as to the wisdom of the concession made in the successive Land Acts for Ireland, which have been passed since 1870 he is much less disquieted, I think, by those concessions, than by the spirit by which the legislation granting them has been guided. He thinks great good has been already done by Mr Balfour, and that much more good will be done by him if the Irish people are made to feel that clamorous resistance to the law will no longer be regarded at Westminster as a sufficient reason for changing the law. That is as much as to say that party spirit in Great Britain is the chief peril of Ireland today. And how can any Irishman, no matter what his state in his own country may be, or his knowledge of Irish affairs, or his patriotic earnestness and desire for Irish prosperity, hope to control the tides of party spirit in England or Scotland?"

I have quoted this author at length because he gives an excellent insight into Arthur's state of mind – and also how he lived in his last years. He was still active, still hunted and still torn between wanting to find solutions and his sense of grievance.

In 1886 and 1887, Kavanagh sent long letters to *The Times* in which he commented on how the situation had changed, and not for the better.

As the 1880s reached their end, things did not improve. *Blackwoods Magazine* also reflected on the irony that Unionist newspapers often did not have correspondents in parts of Ireland like Tipperary but took the news from Parnellite papers, news that was obviously heavily slanted in favour of the Fenians.

It is hardly surprising that these repetitive battles should depress Arthur, but as in the past, he fell back on what he called 'the consolations of the sea'. In 1888, he sailed again on his new boat the *Water Lily* but he fell ill and they came back to Borris. Later, he developed bronchial trouble but it cleared up and in July 1889, he was well enough to set sail with Frances for Holland. They visited Amsterdam and Flushing. Arthur felt better and he shot what would turn out to be the last 'bag' of his life. It consisted of eight ducks and two wigeon.

In the autumn Arthur and Frances stayed in their house in Tedworth Square. Arthur was getting more and more ill. He knew it and so did his wife and their children. On Christmas Eve his family gathered round his bed. They sang Christmas carols and Frances sat up with him throughout the night. The end was peaceful. Arthur Kavanagh died on Christmas morning surrounded by all those who loved him and who he loved best.

The obituaries

At the start of this book I suggested that many writers have complained that the disabled tend to get written out of history: history that is written by the able-bodied, after all. In Arthur's case that was surprisingly true given the very considerable role he played in public life. *The Times* astonishingly did not carry an obituary notice.

The *Illustrated London News* said that Arthur 'has always been staunch and steady, ever ready to defend Irish interests and to give his assistance to all measures tending to the interests of his country.'

The *Edinburgh Magazine* carried a longer account of his life and highlighted the ways in which he had overcome his 'impossibles'. The medical journal, *The Lancet*, recorded his death but dealt with it more as a medical case history than a human triumph.

I have studied Arthur on and off for 8 years. The more I study him the more I am convinced he was a remarkable man whose history has lessons for us today. It is astonishing and scandalous that his achievements – not to mention his escapades – have been forgotten. I hope this book does something to help him find the place he deserves in the history both of Britain and Ireland.

Selected bibliography

Ackroyd P. (2002) *Dickens*, Vintage, London.

Anon. (1841) *The Reign of Terror in Carlow*, British Library.

Bull G. (1981) Facial disfigurement, *Psychology News*, **7**.

Comerford R.V. (1998) *The Fenians in Context*, Merlin Publishing.

Edmonds D. and Eidinow J. (1990) *Wittgenstein's Poker*, Faber & Faber, London.

Erikson E. (1995) *Identity and the Life Cycle*, W.W Norton, New York.

Fisher S. and Cleveland S. (1969) *Body Image and Personality*, Dover Publications, New York.

Fraser M. (1973) *Children in Conflict*, Penguin, Harmondsworth, UK.

Froebel F. (2003) *The Autobiography of Friedrich Froebel*, University of Pacific Press, Hawaii.

Hardyment C. (1995) *Perfect Parents*, Oxford Paperbacks, Oxford, UK.

Goman I. (1963) *Stigma: The Management of Spoiled Identity*, Penguin, Harmondsworth, UK.

Gouin de Cardie (1971) *A Follow-up Study in the Mental and Emotional Development of Thalidomide Children and the Mother's Reaction*, Rehabilitation Institute of Montreal.

Kavanagh K. (1989) *Born without Limbs*, private publication.

Lee H. (1979) *The Wild Boy of Aveyron*, Cambridge University Press, Cambridge, UK.

Macarthy M. (1936) *Six Handicaps*, Longmans Green, London.

Maitland S. (1983) *Vesta Tilley*, Virago, London.

Marland H. (2003) *Dangerous Motherhood: Insanity and Childbirth in Victorian Britain*, Palgrave, London.

McCormick D. (1960) *The Incredible Mr Kavanagh*, Putnam, London.

McWhirter L. and Trew K. (1987) *In the Power of Psychology*, Croom Helm, Beckenham, UK [edited by David Cohen].

Montague Ashley (1970) *The Elephant Man*, Alison & Busby, London.

Pestalozzi H. (1824) *A Book for the People*.

Pestalozzi H. (1827) *Letters of Early Education*.

Piaget J. (1952) *Origins of Intelligence in Children*, Routledge & Kegan Paul, London.

Plumb J.H. (1963) *England in the 18th Century*, Penguin, Harmondsworth, UK.

Putti V. (1930) *The History of Artificial Limbs*, New York.

Phillips G. (1990) *Best Foot Forward*, Granta Publications, Cambridge, UK.

Seligman M. (1995) *Learned Optimism*, Free Press, New York.

Steele, Sarah (1891) *Arthur Kavanagh*, Macmillan, London.

Unthan E. (1935) *The Armless Fiddler*, George Allen & Unwin, London.

Wood, Gaby (1998) *The Smallest of All Persons Mentioned in the Records of Littleness*, Profile Books, London.

4/22